BAMUSERS 2
MORE MUSINGS IN ART

BRUCE ARLEN

ArlenArts
Cave Creek

BAMUSERS 2: MORE MUSINGS IN ART

Author: Bruce Arlen
Cover and Book Design: Marty Safir, Double M Graphics

Published by

ArlenArts
P.O. Box 4023
Cave Creek, Arizona 85327

www.bamusers.com

ISBN 978-0-9913007-4-7

9 8 7 6 5 4 3 2 1

For Sam & Kaia, with Love
The Beginning

It's time to unleash a new brigade of Bamusers. They've bristled at confinement waiting for expression, and now as they march in rhythm, they're reaching out to you in the ways that they do so that you might enjoy them in the ways that you do.

Good luck!

Bruce Arlen

Bruce Arlen

BAMUSERS 2

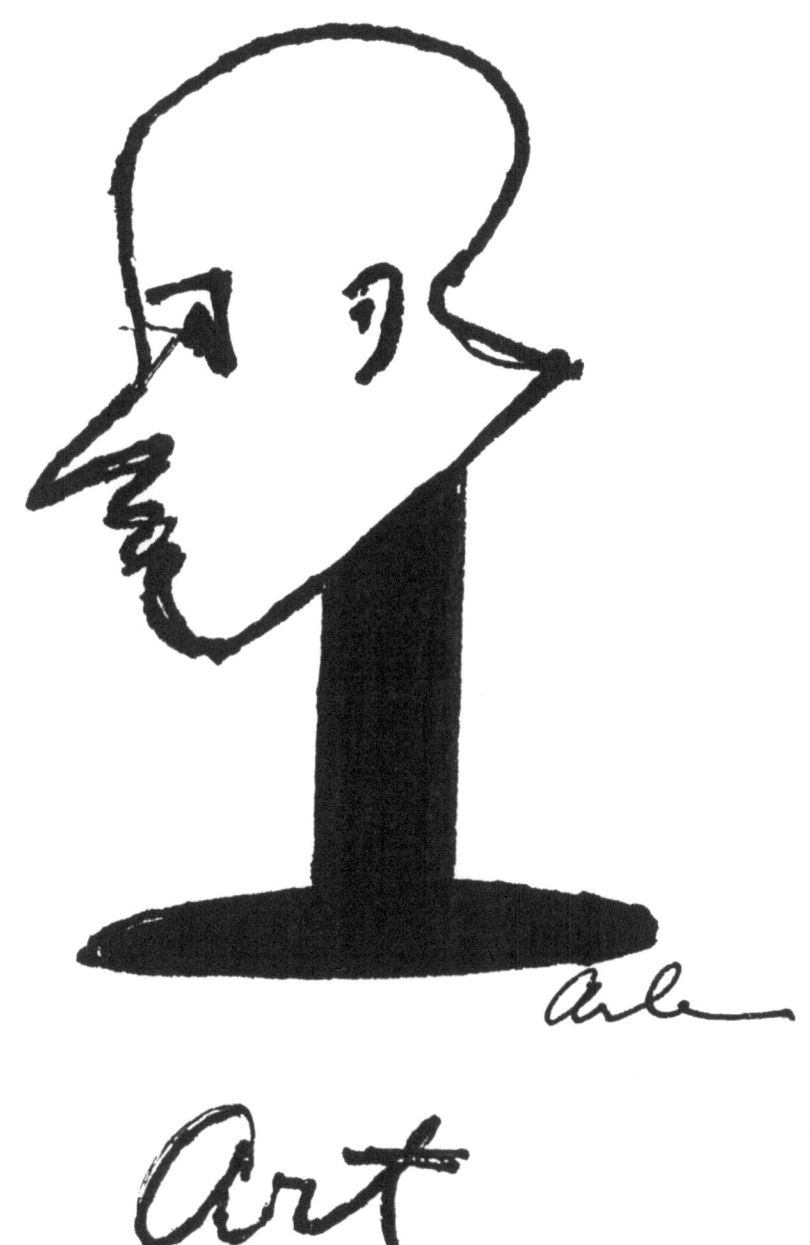

Art

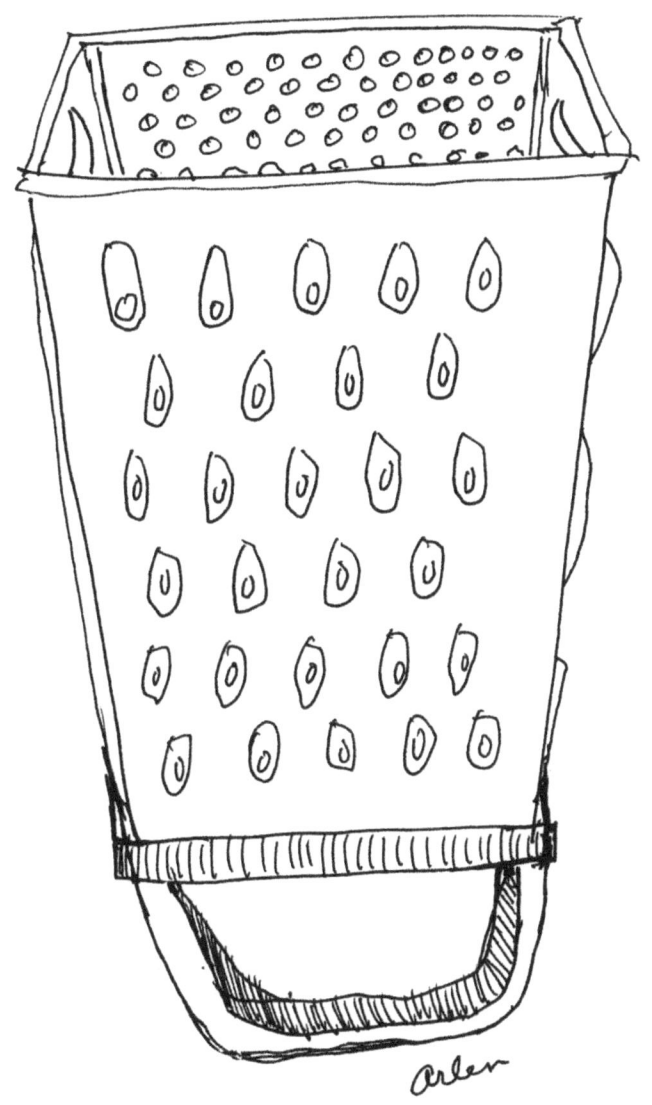

Frederick the . . . .

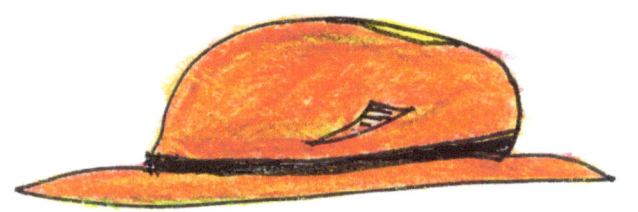

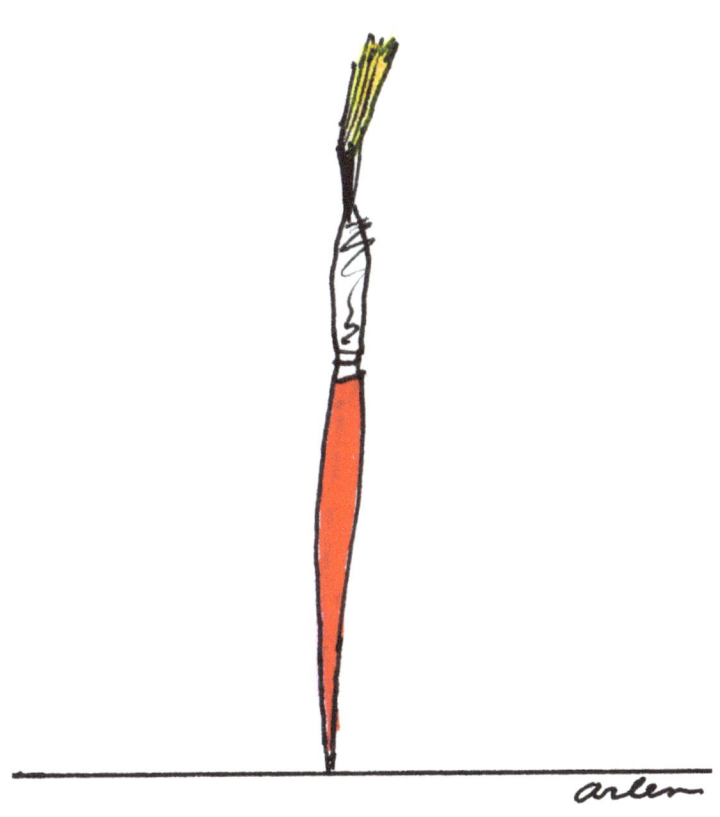

URBAN ART

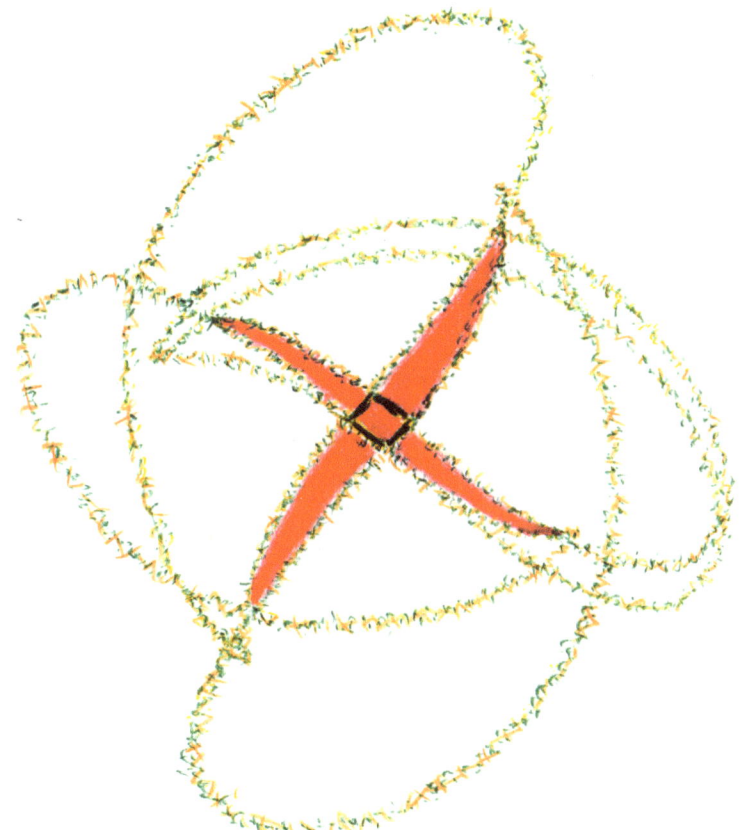

Santa's Belt Galaxy
arlen

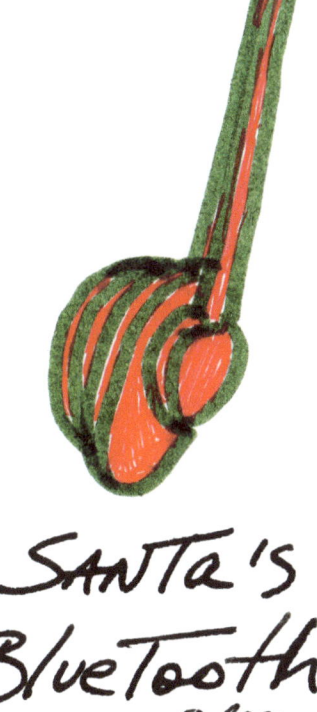

SANTA'S
BlueTooth
arlen

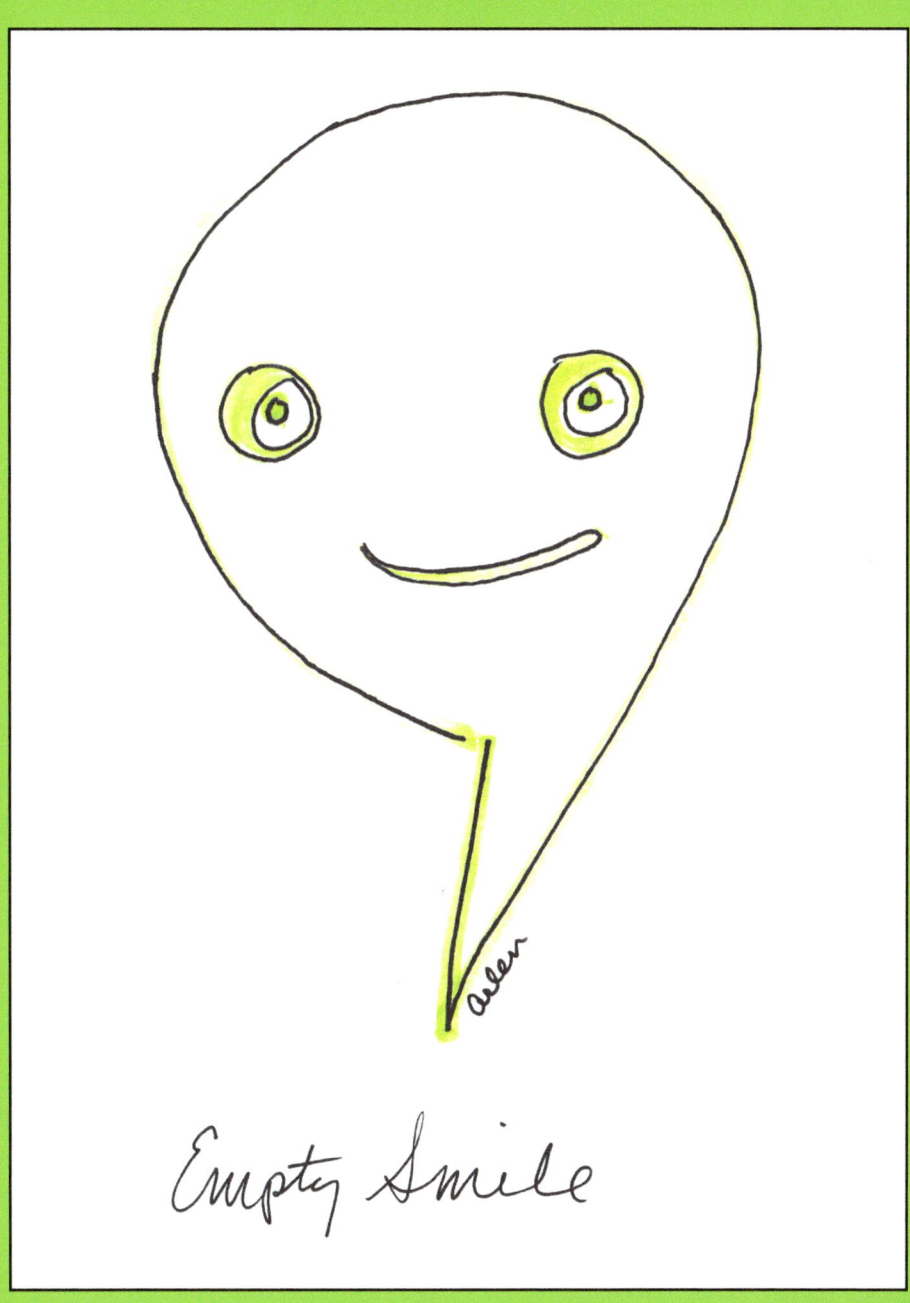

Empty Smile

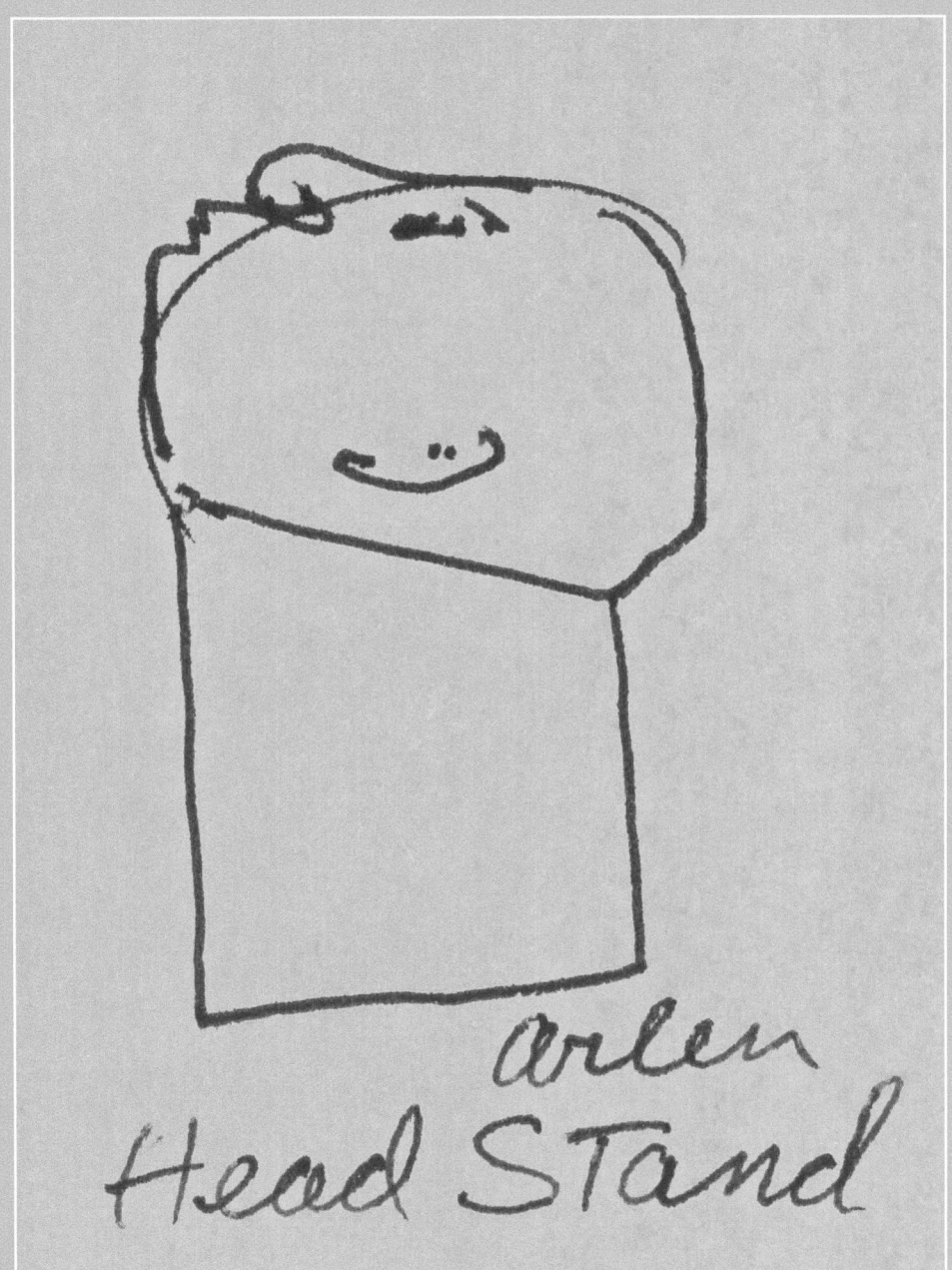

arlen
Head Stand

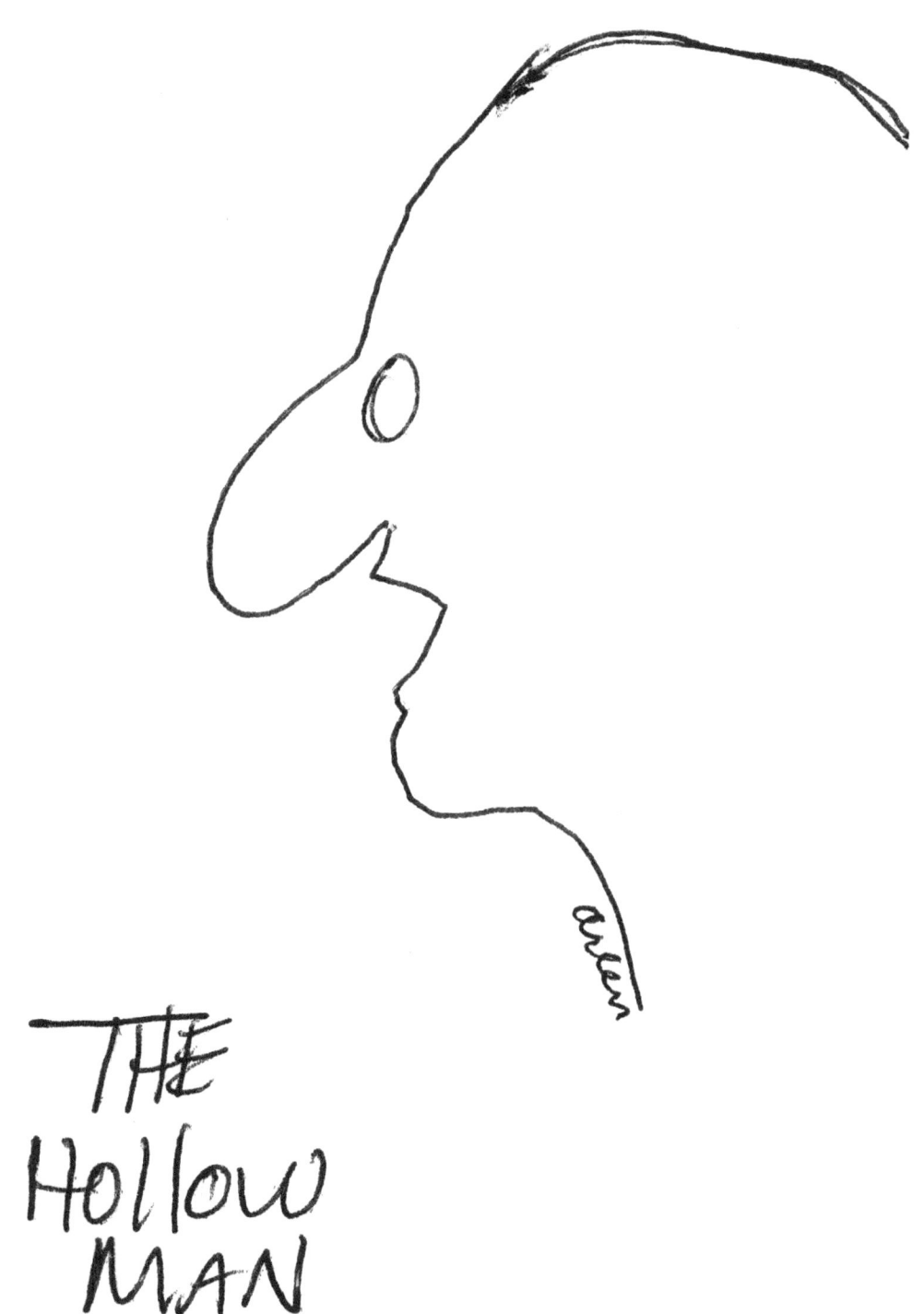

THE
HOLLOW
MAN

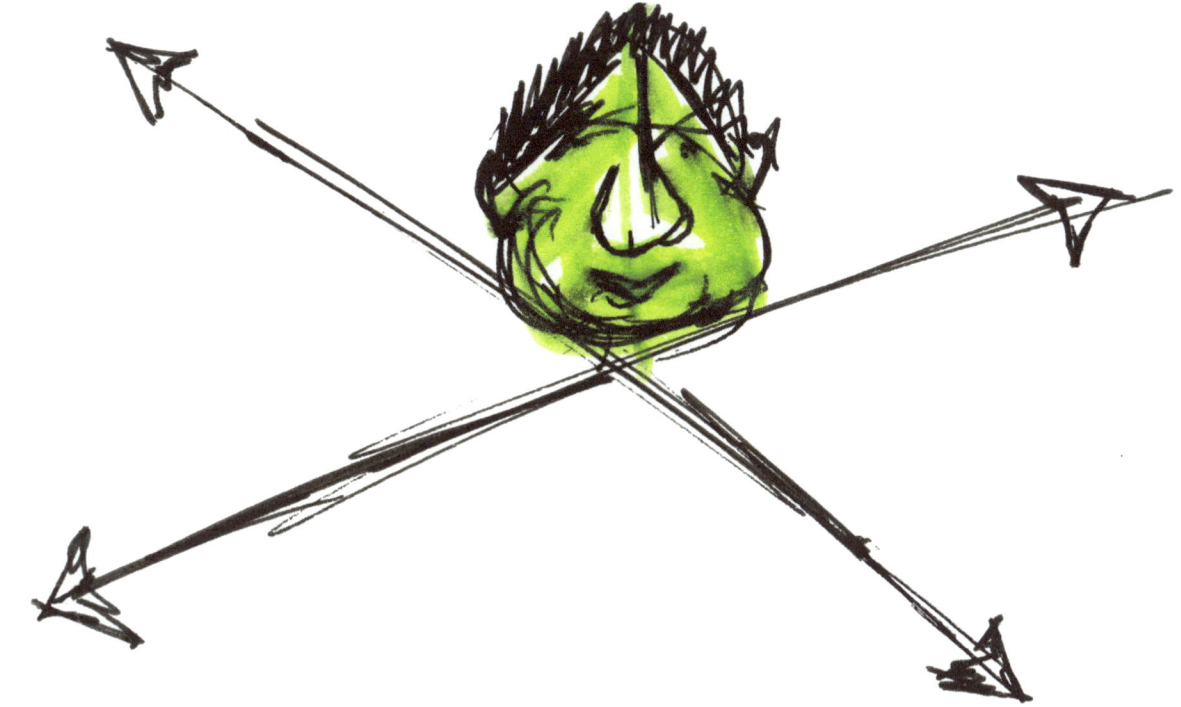

MURRAY'S COAT OF ARMS

Arlen

So I only need cleaning every 6 months now?

Arlen

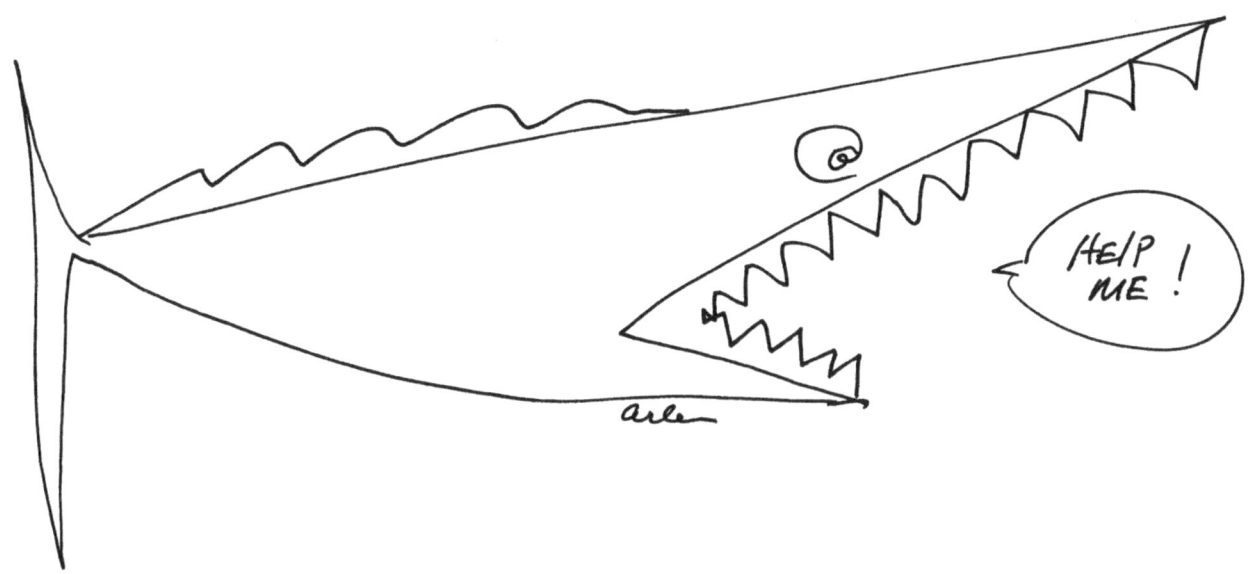

BAD CASE OF LOCKJAW

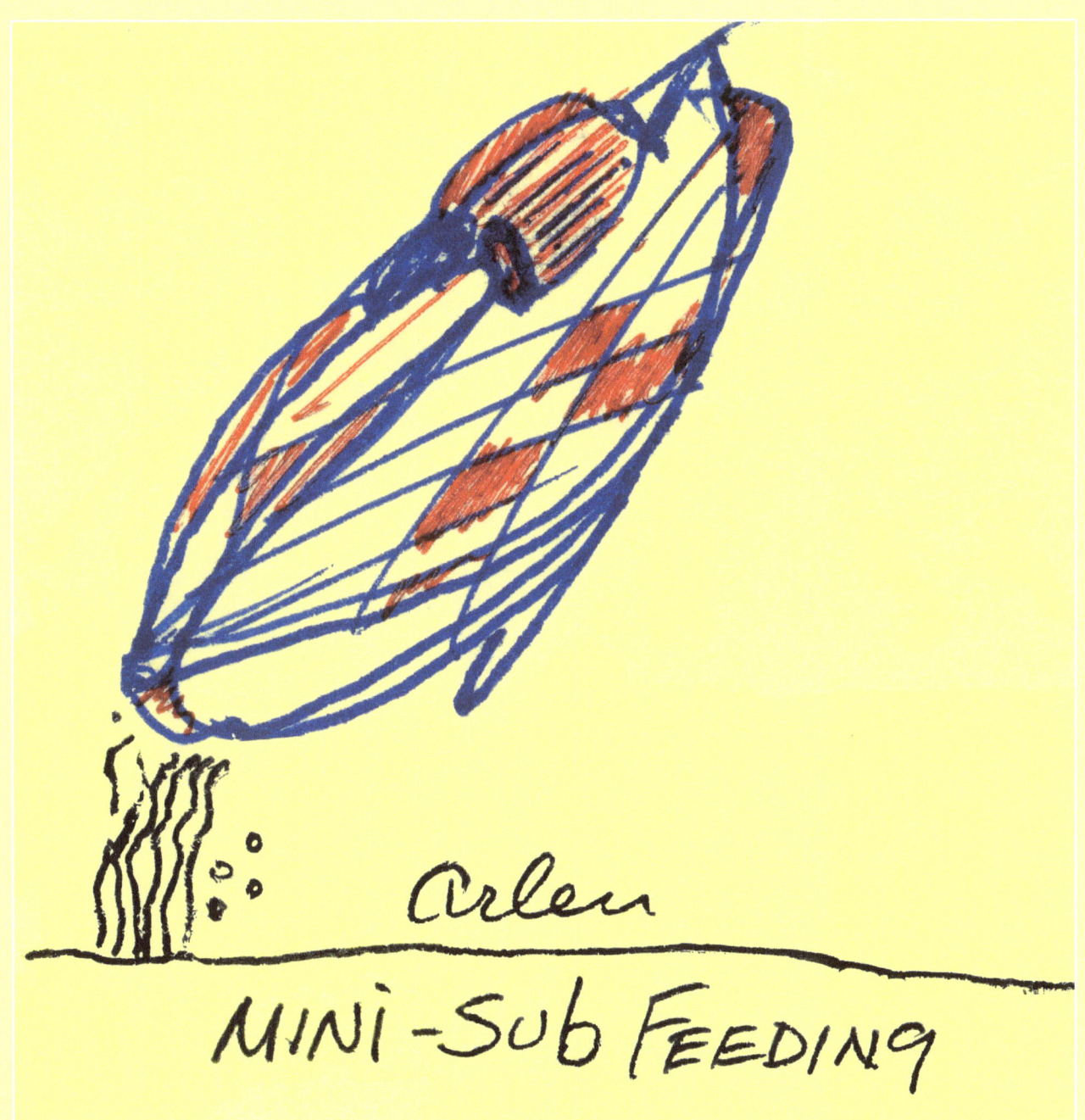

arlen

MINI-SUB FEEDING

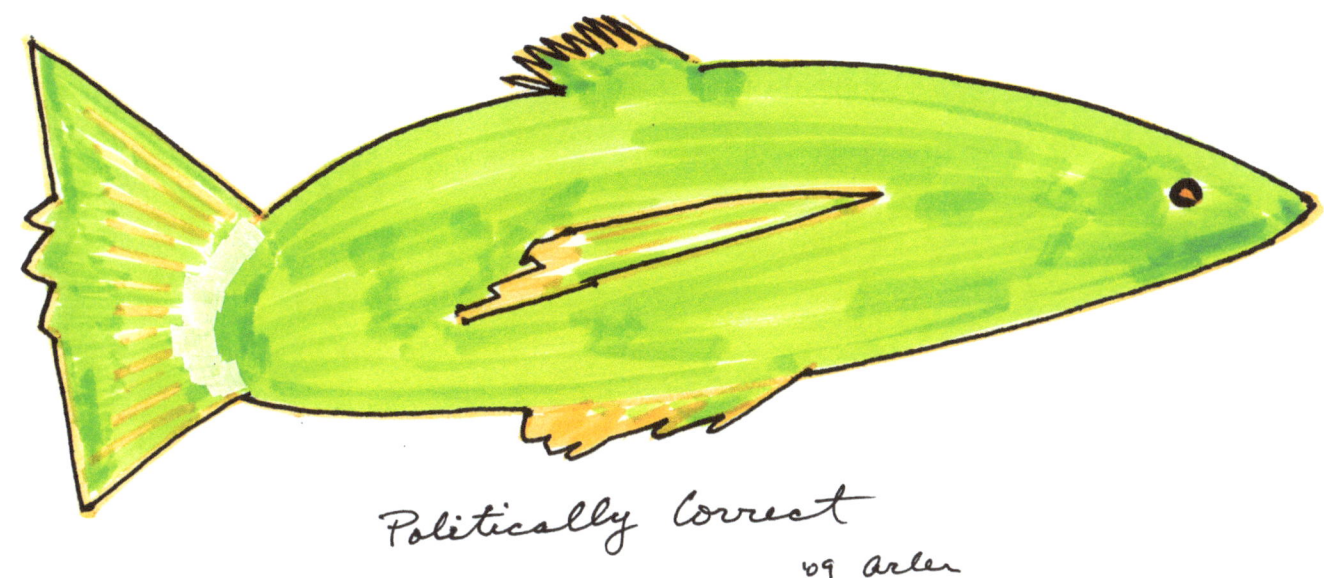

Politically Correct
'09 arlen

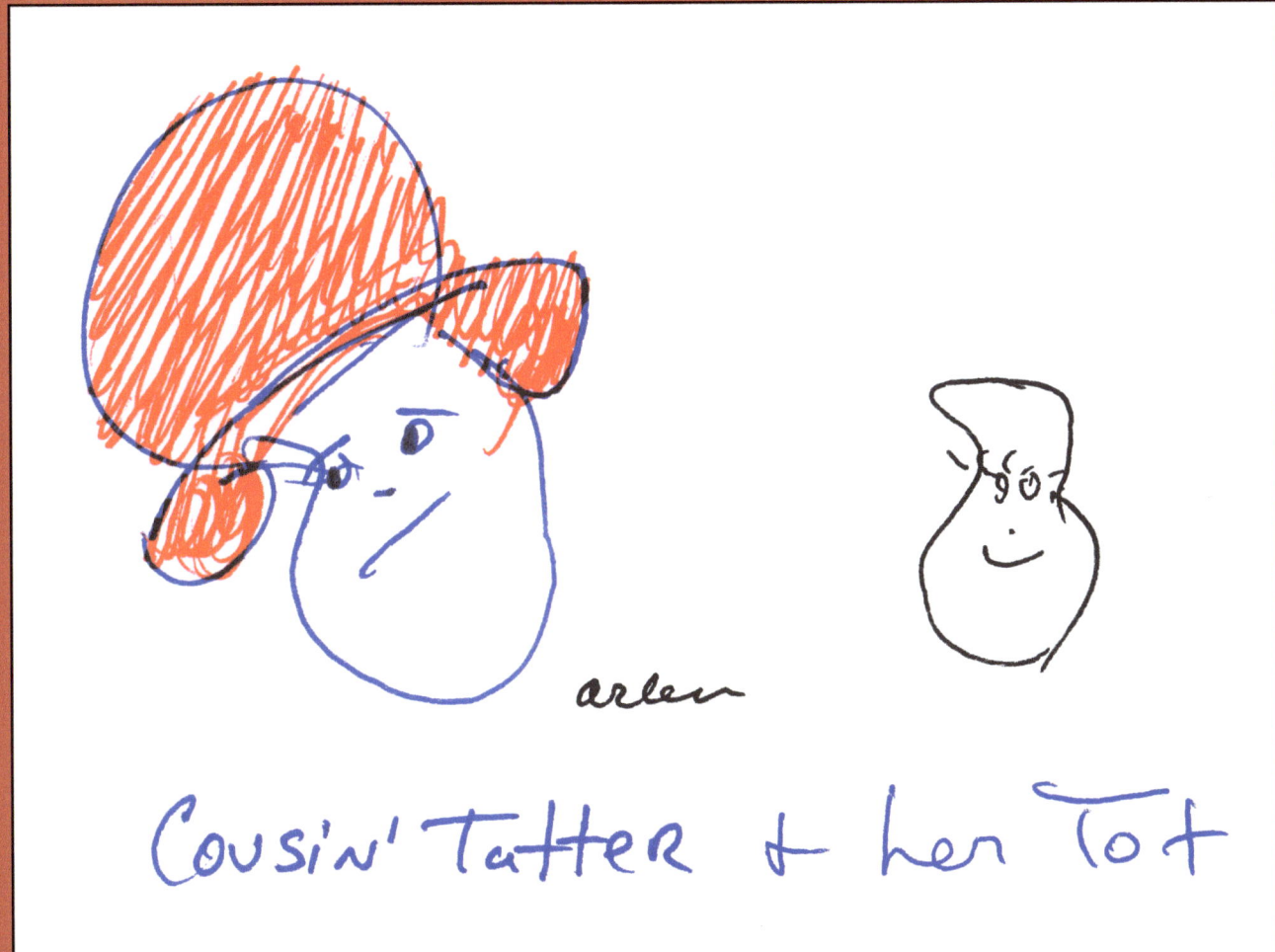

Brush Man & Friend
arlen

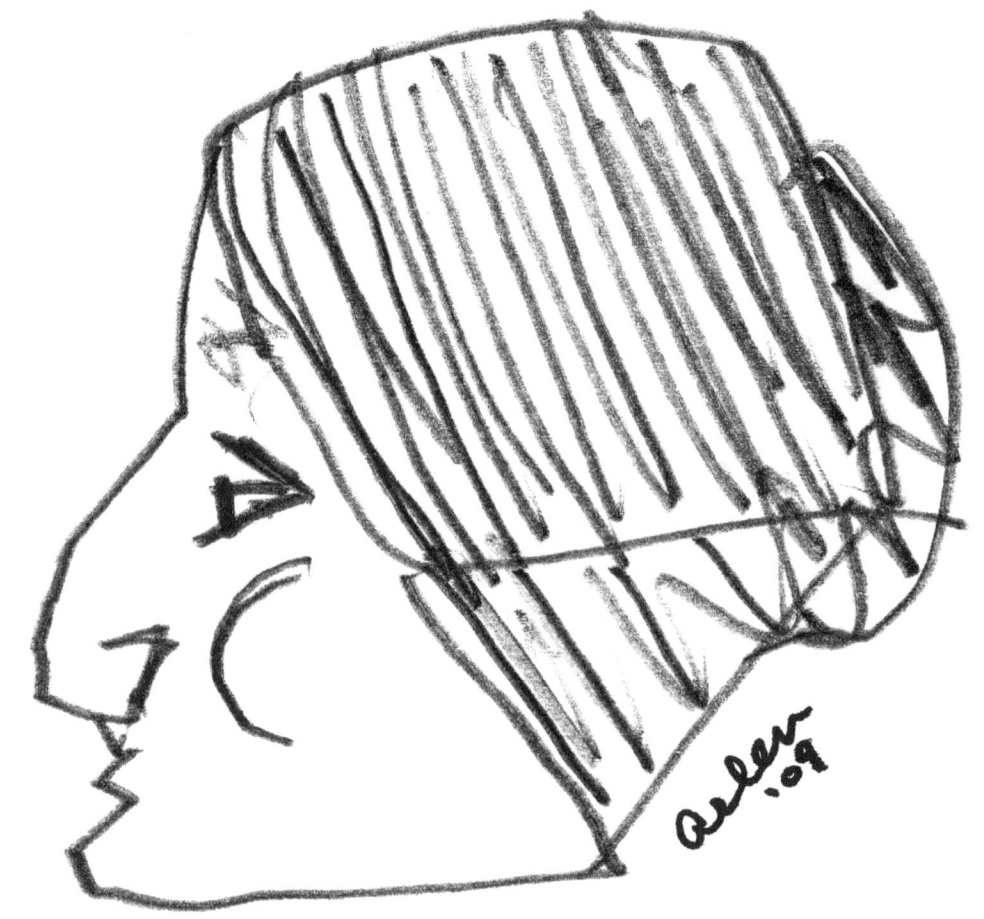

Grandma's got attitude!

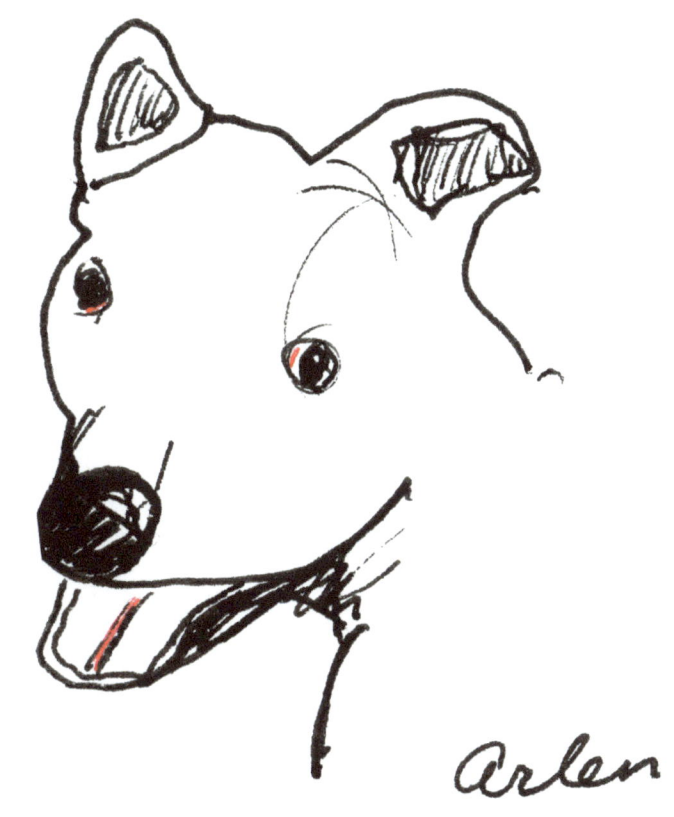

Arlen

CAUTIOUS OPTIMISM

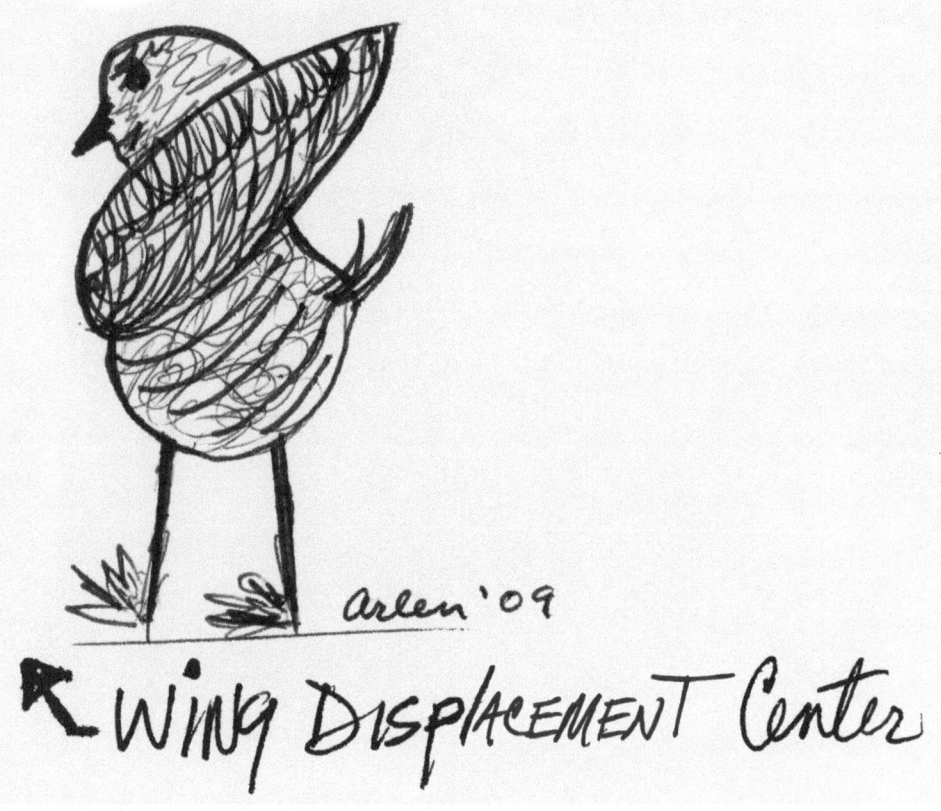

arlen '09

R wing Displacement Center

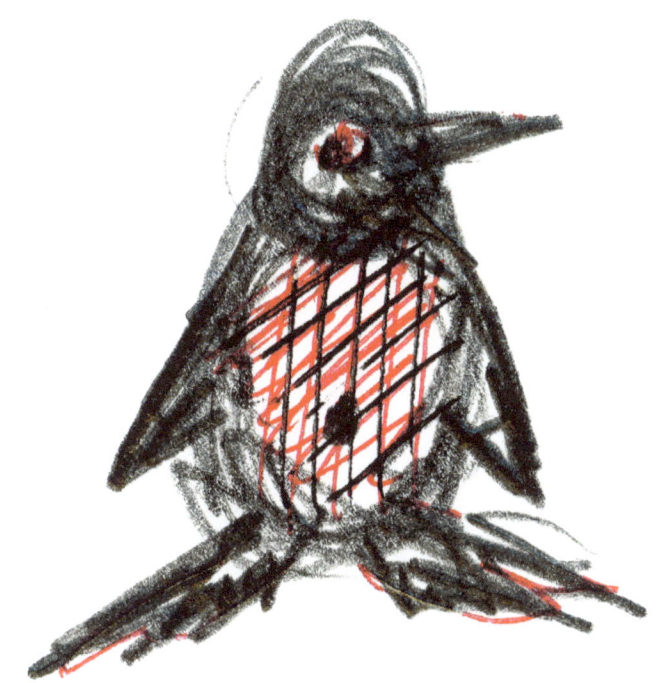

Scottish Penguin
aveen -

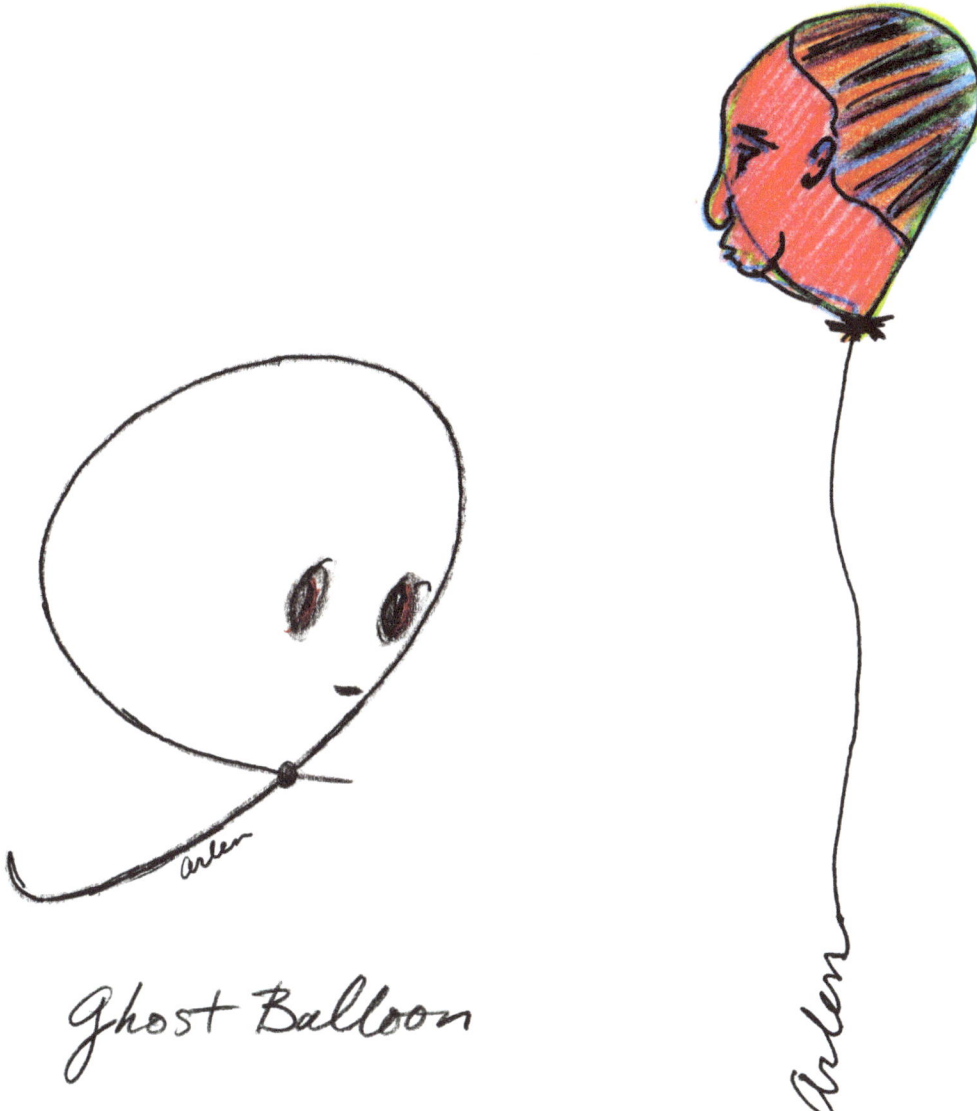

Ghost Balloon

Accountant Balloon.

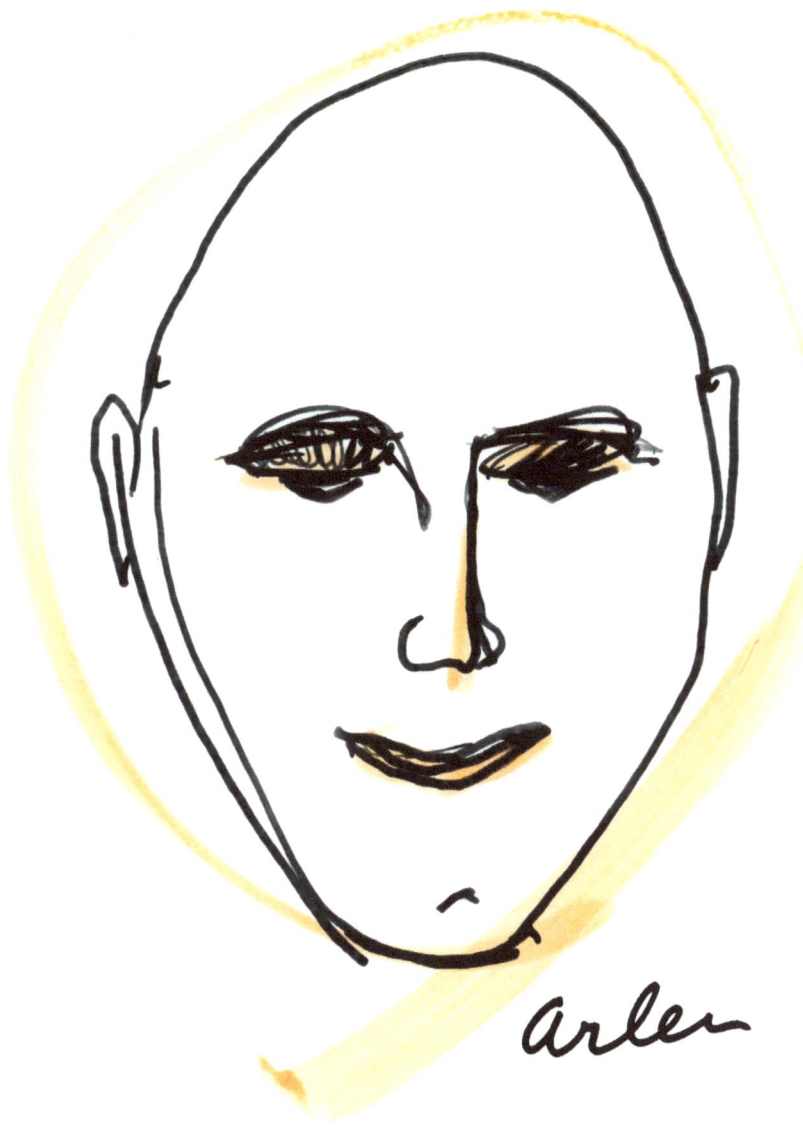

Arlen

THE
MORRIE LISA

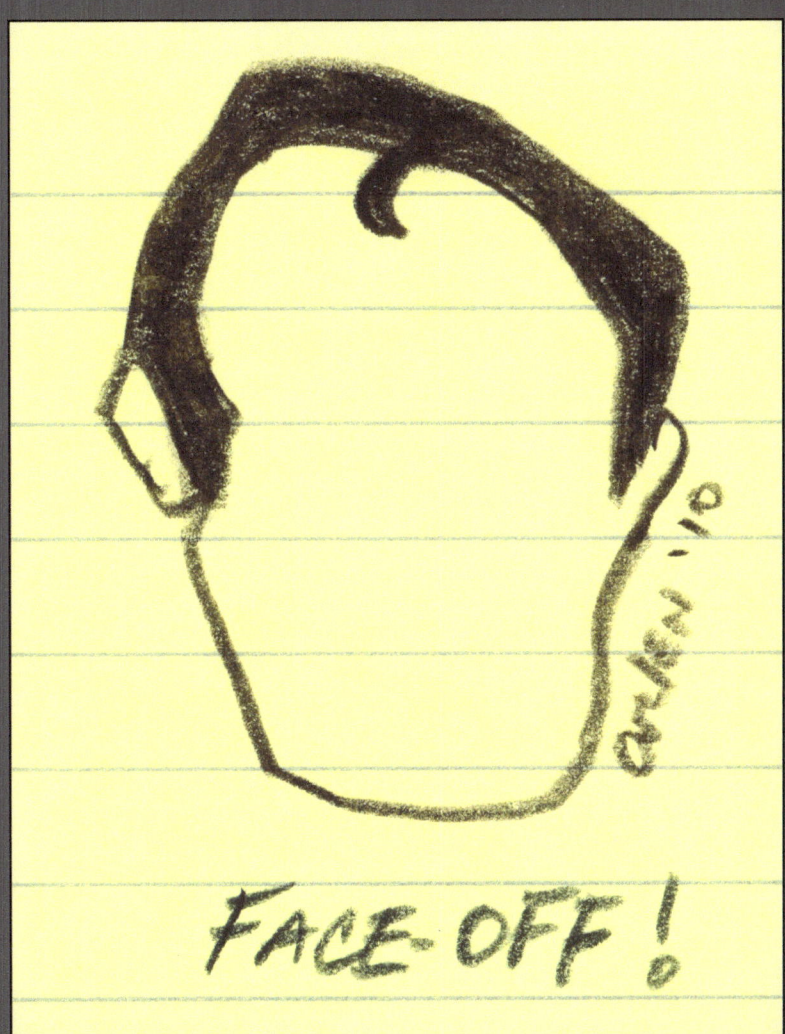

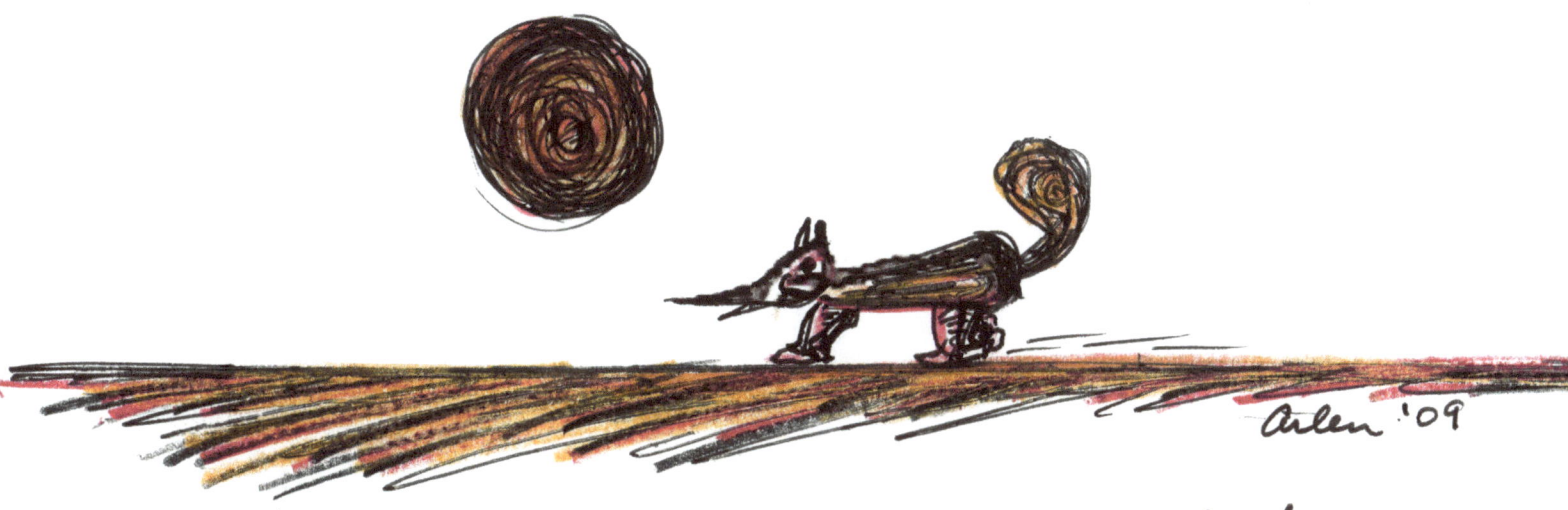

Vice President; Full Moon Society

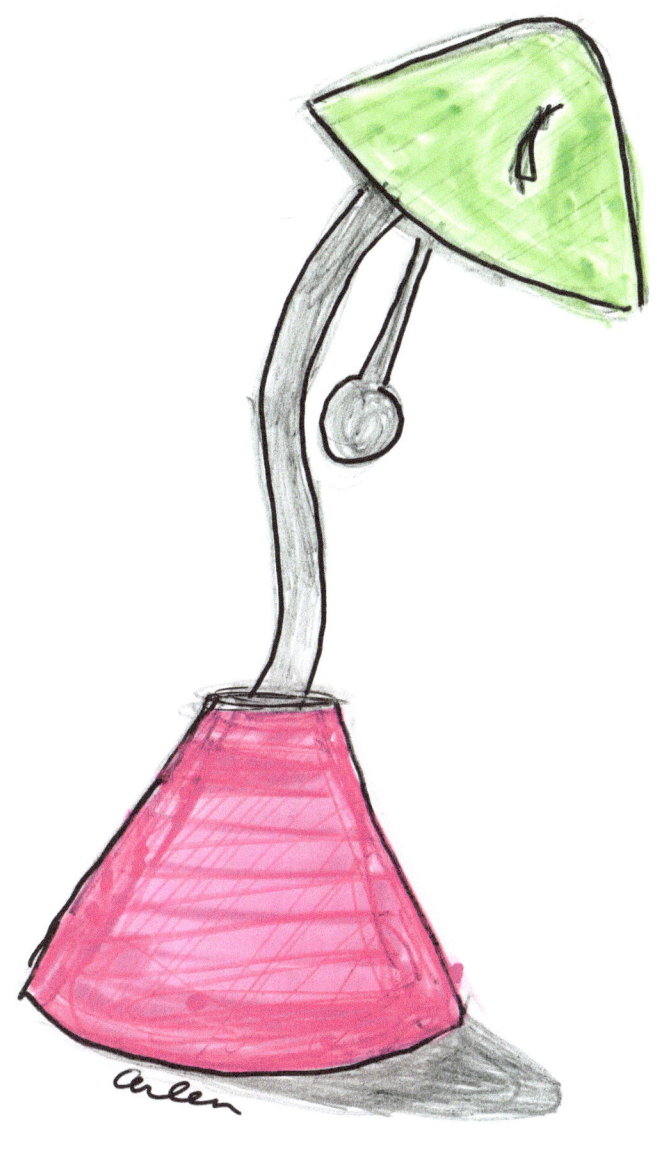

off-Duty

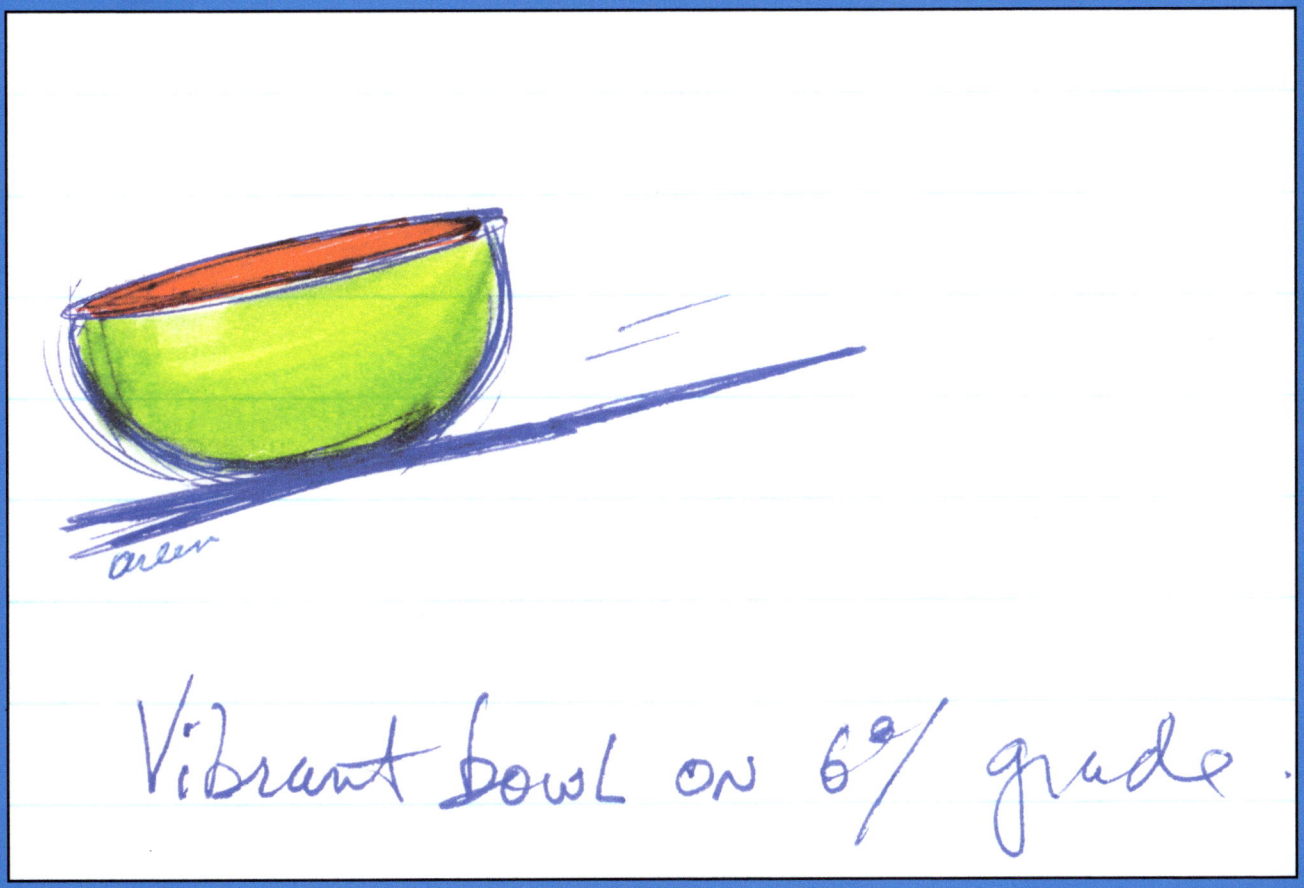

Vibrant bowl on 6% grade.

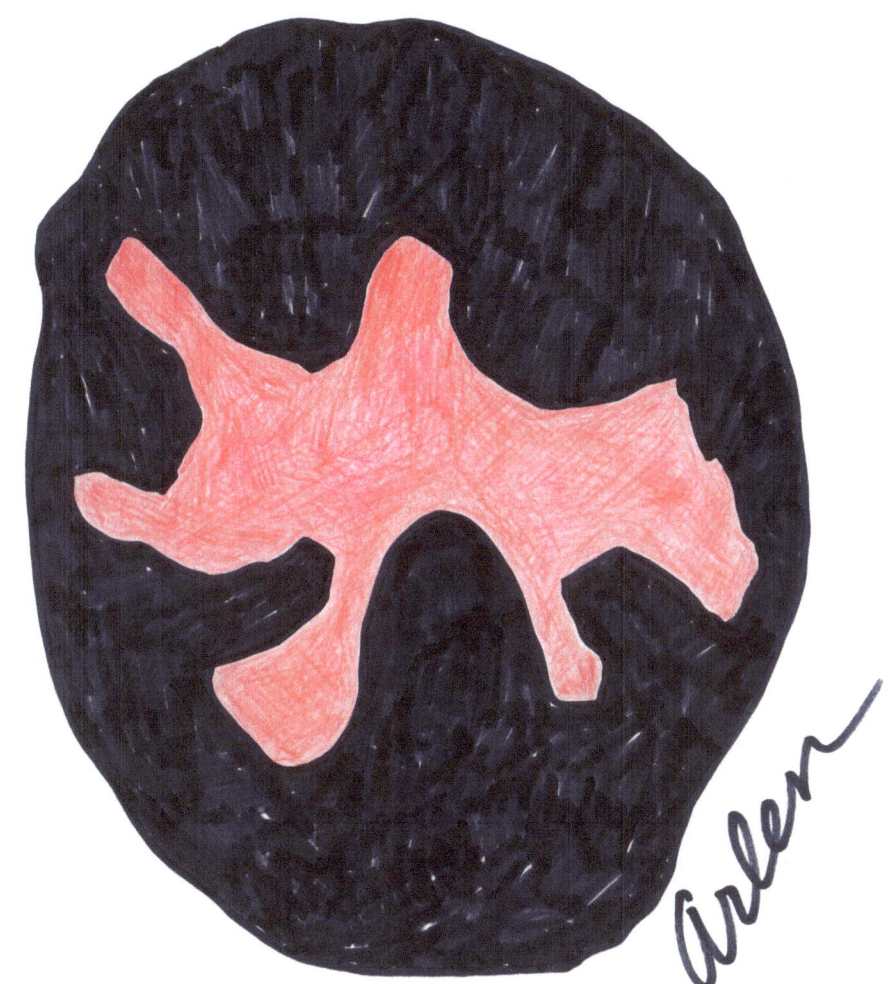

PET.
FOSSIL

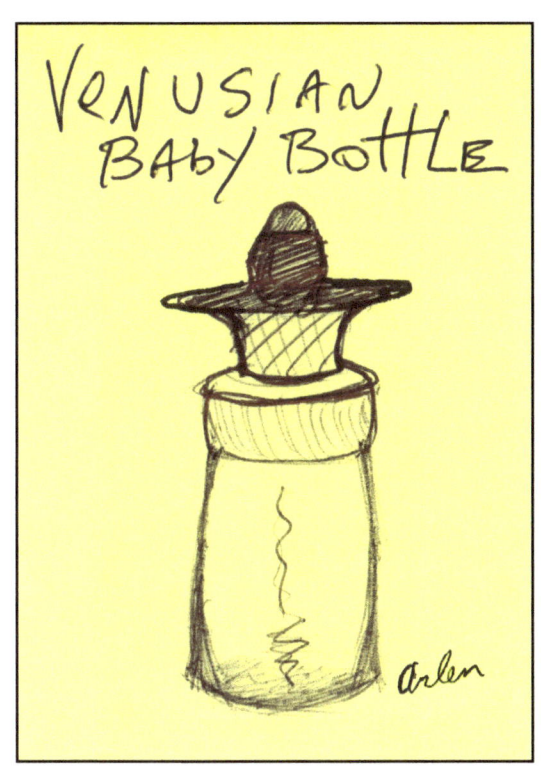

VENUSIAN BABY BOTTLE

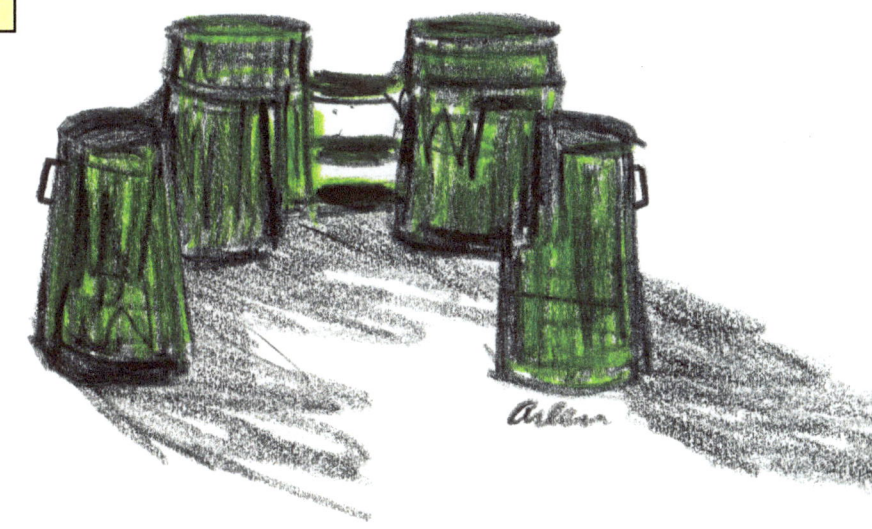

Venusian Quadnoculars

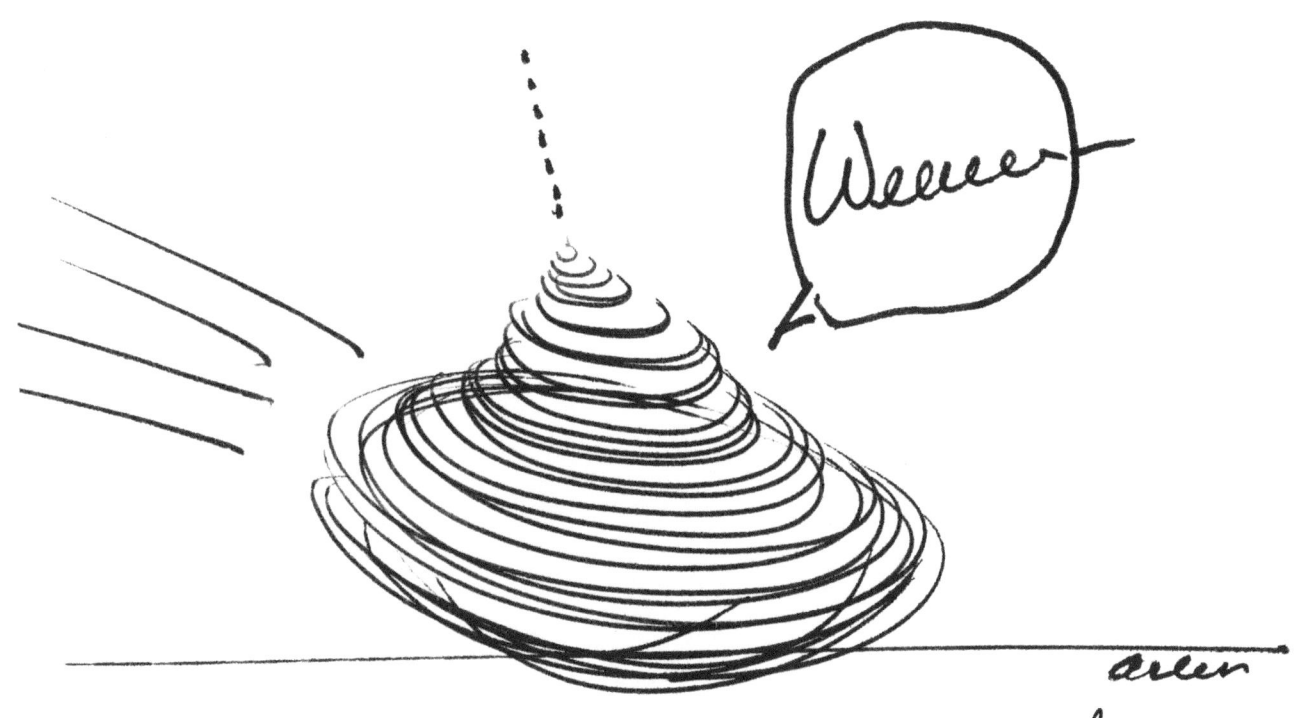

Teen Alien Steals Dad's Saucer

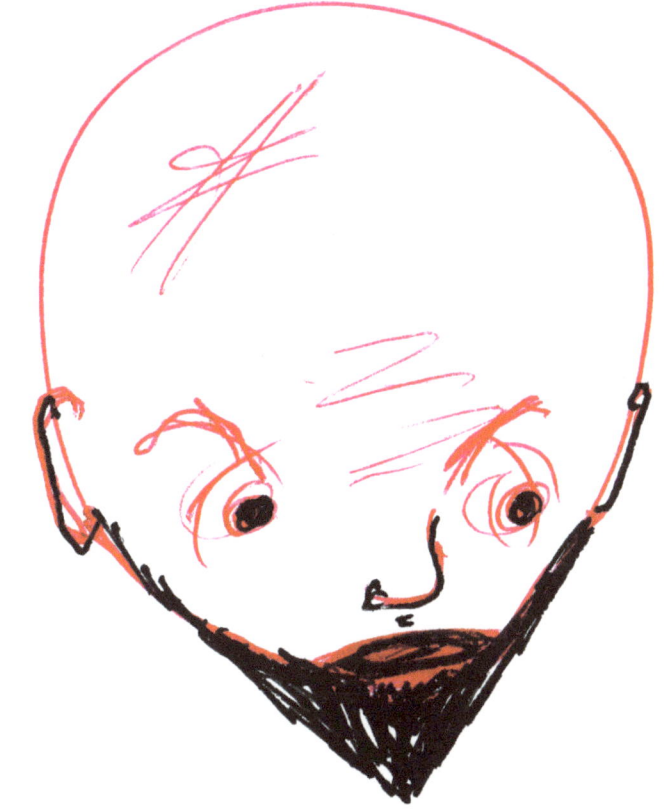

Vladimir Lenin
Age 10

arlen

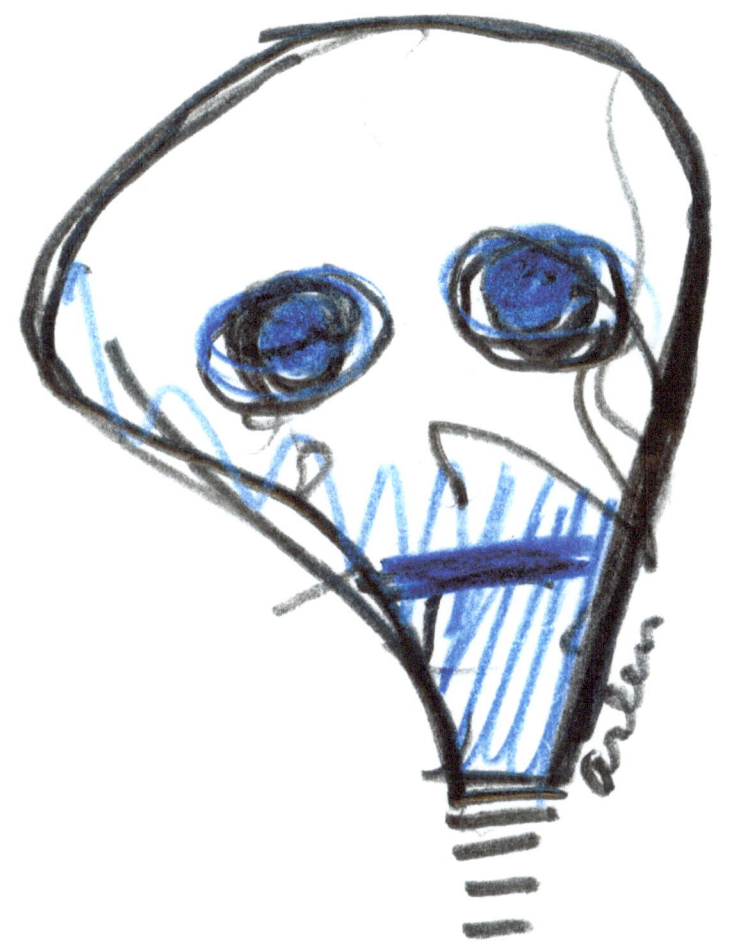

GHost Bulb

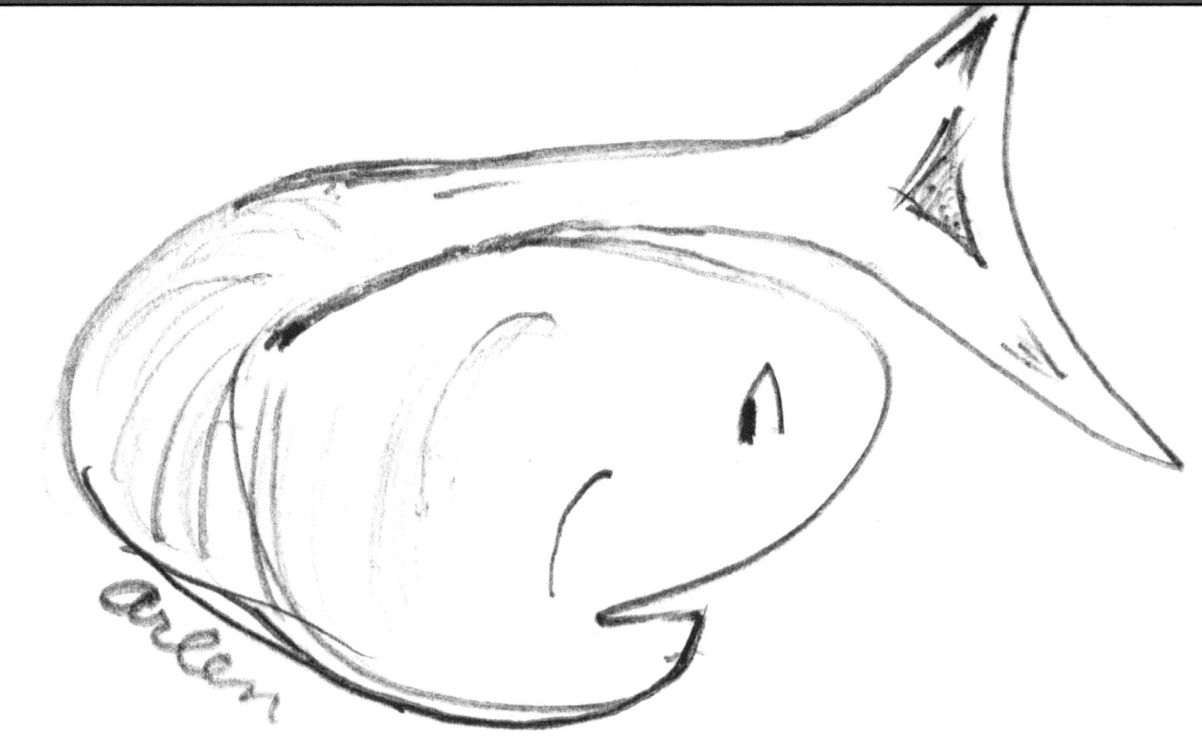

Surprise !!

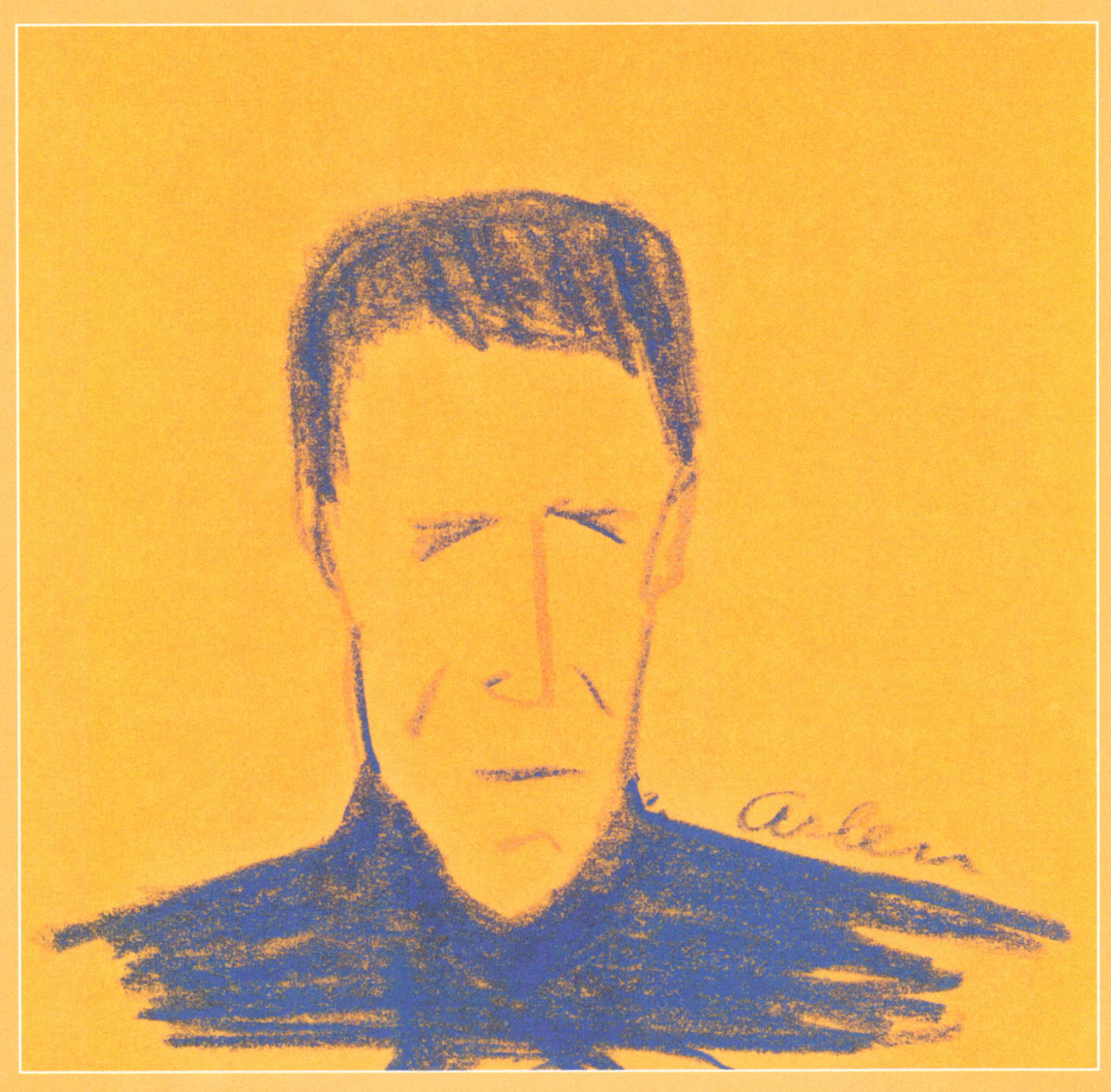

STASH NAPKIN
COFFEE HOUSE DETECTIVE

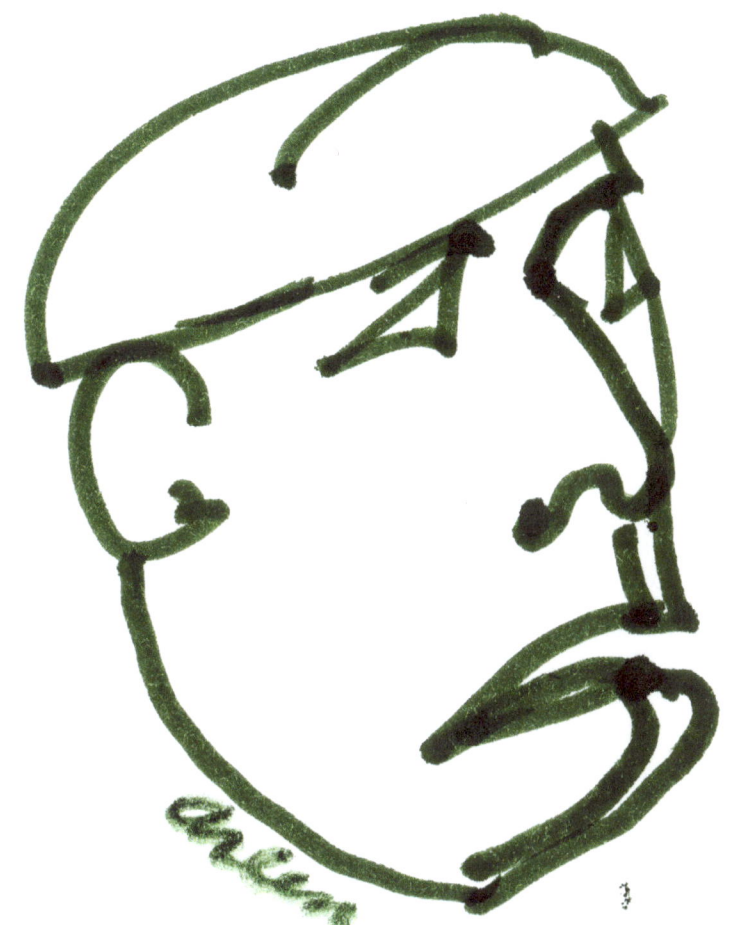

HAIR CUT BOWL
STUCK TO HEAD .

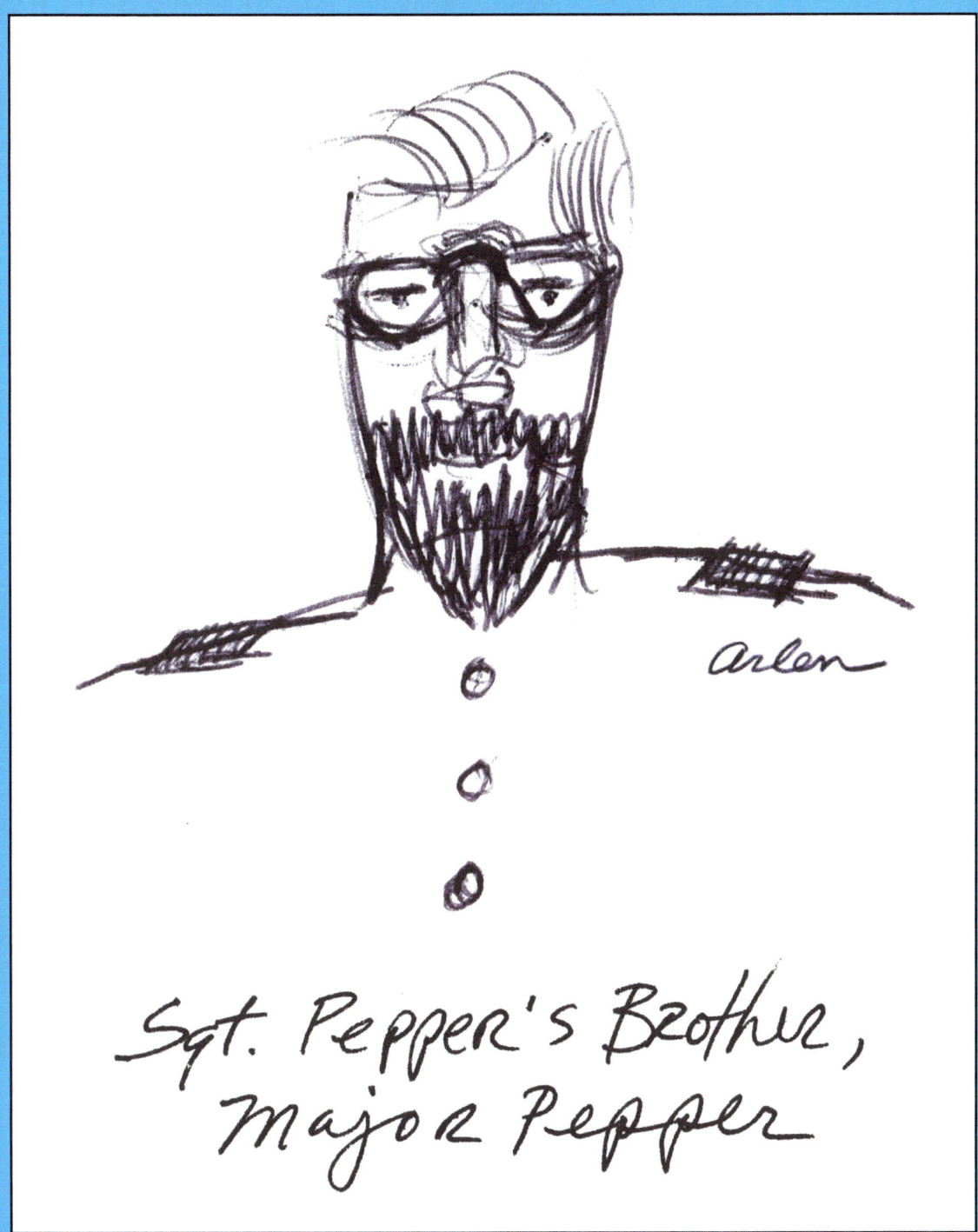

Sgt. Pepper's Brother,
Major Pepper

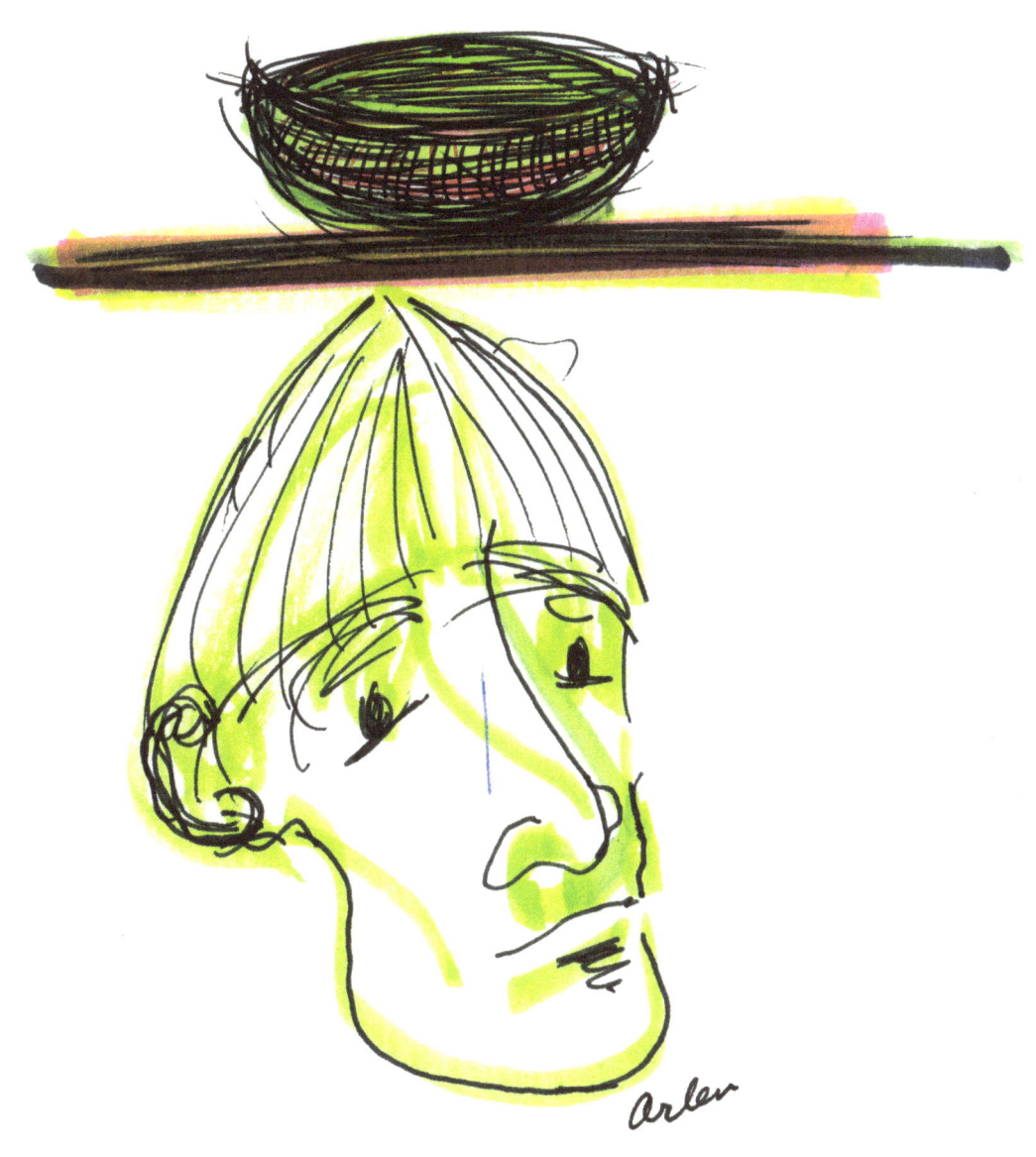

I'M Pre·Columbian ?

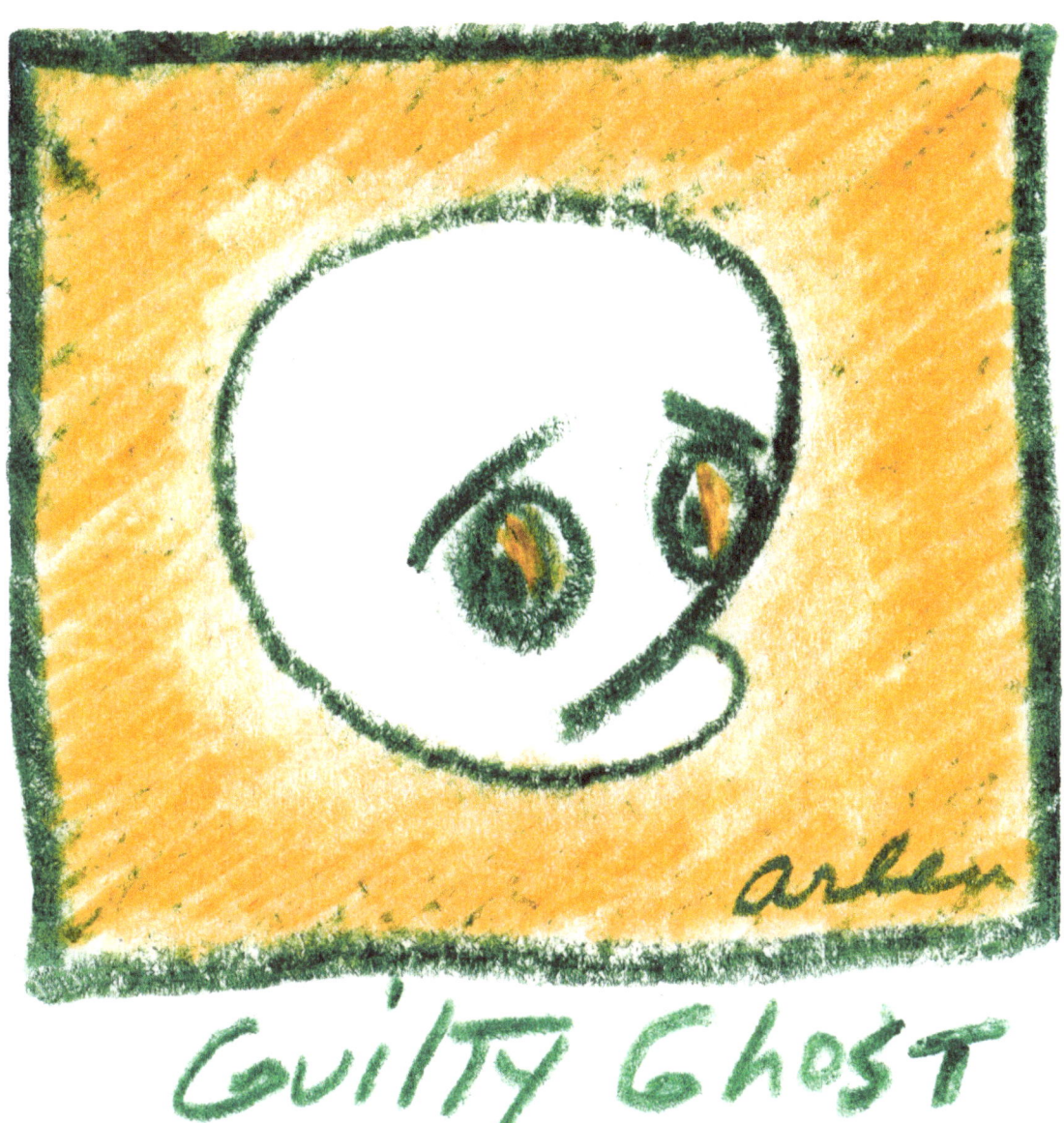

Guilty Ghost

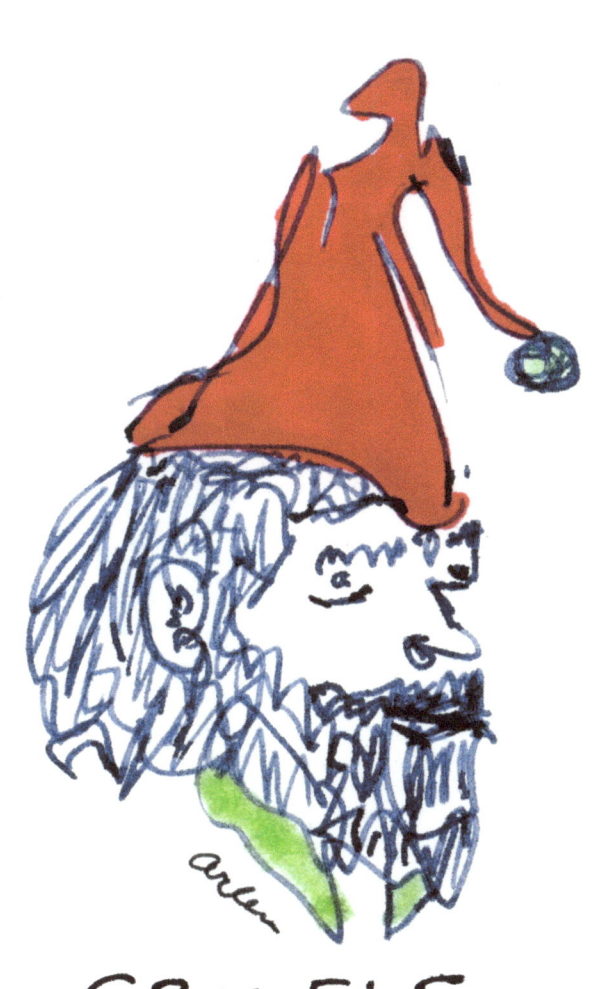

GRIM ELF

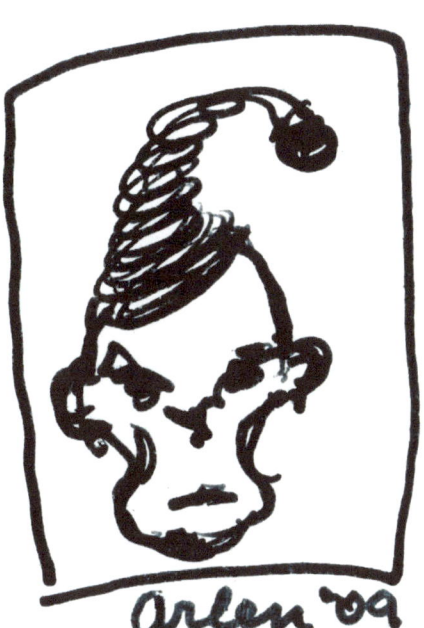

arlen '09

NOT-
A
Jolly
Roger

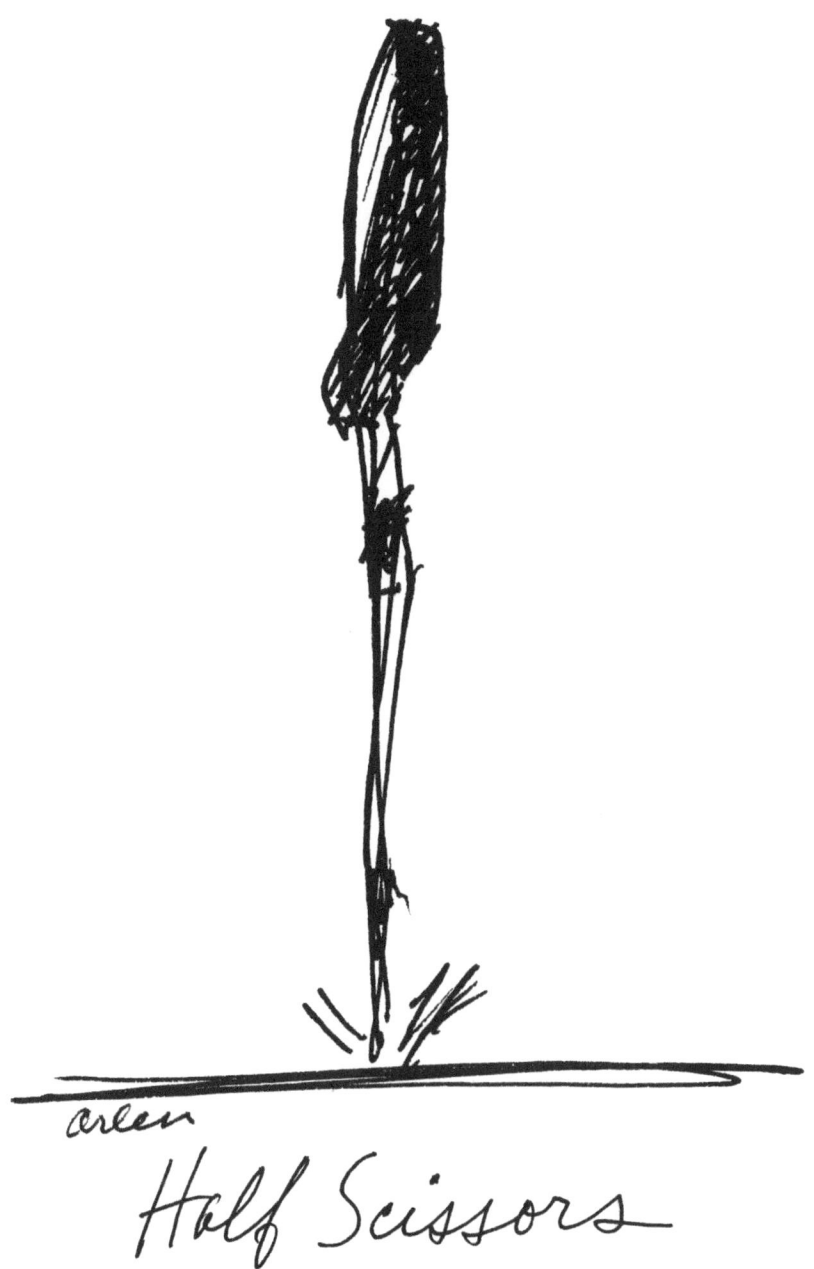

arlen

Half Scissors
Standing

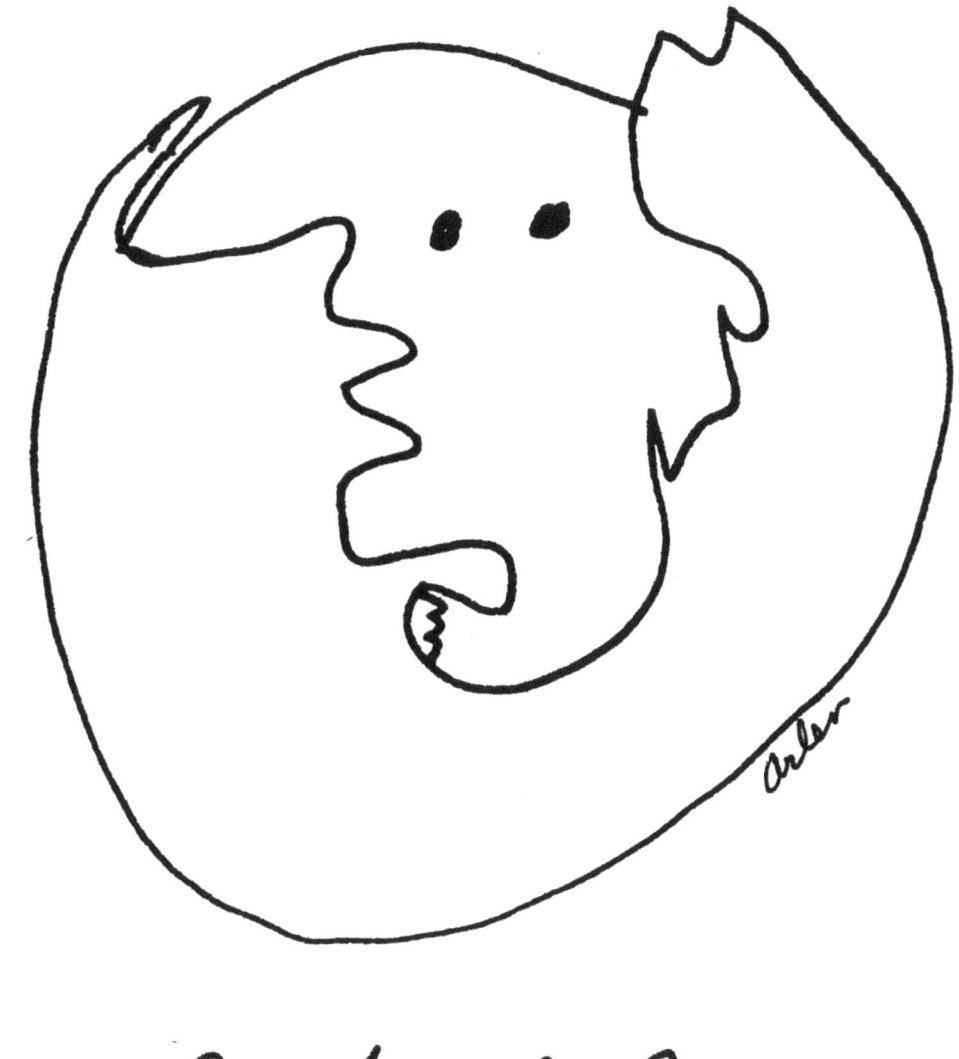

Elephant Egg

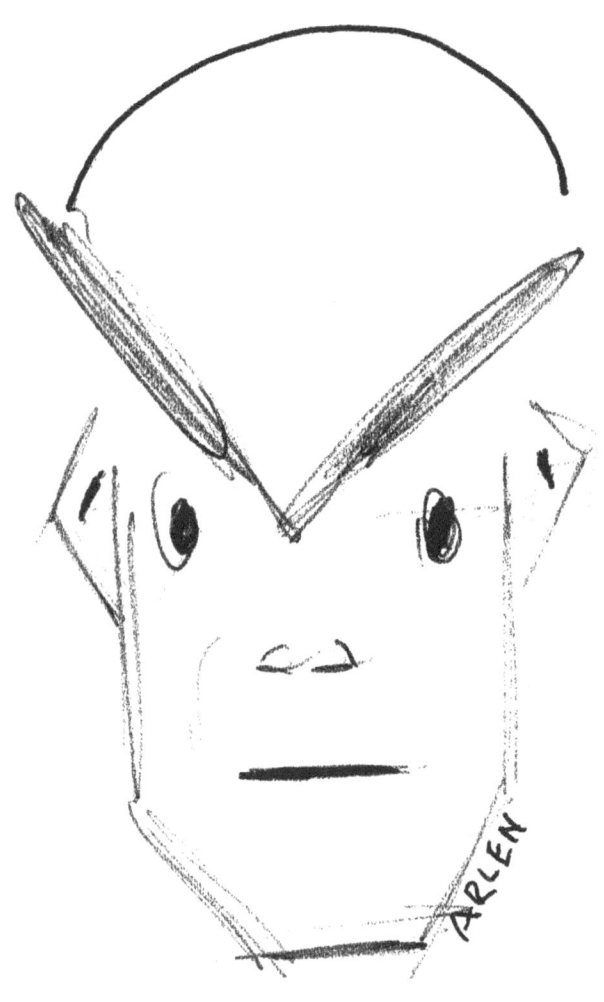

ART DECO ALIEN

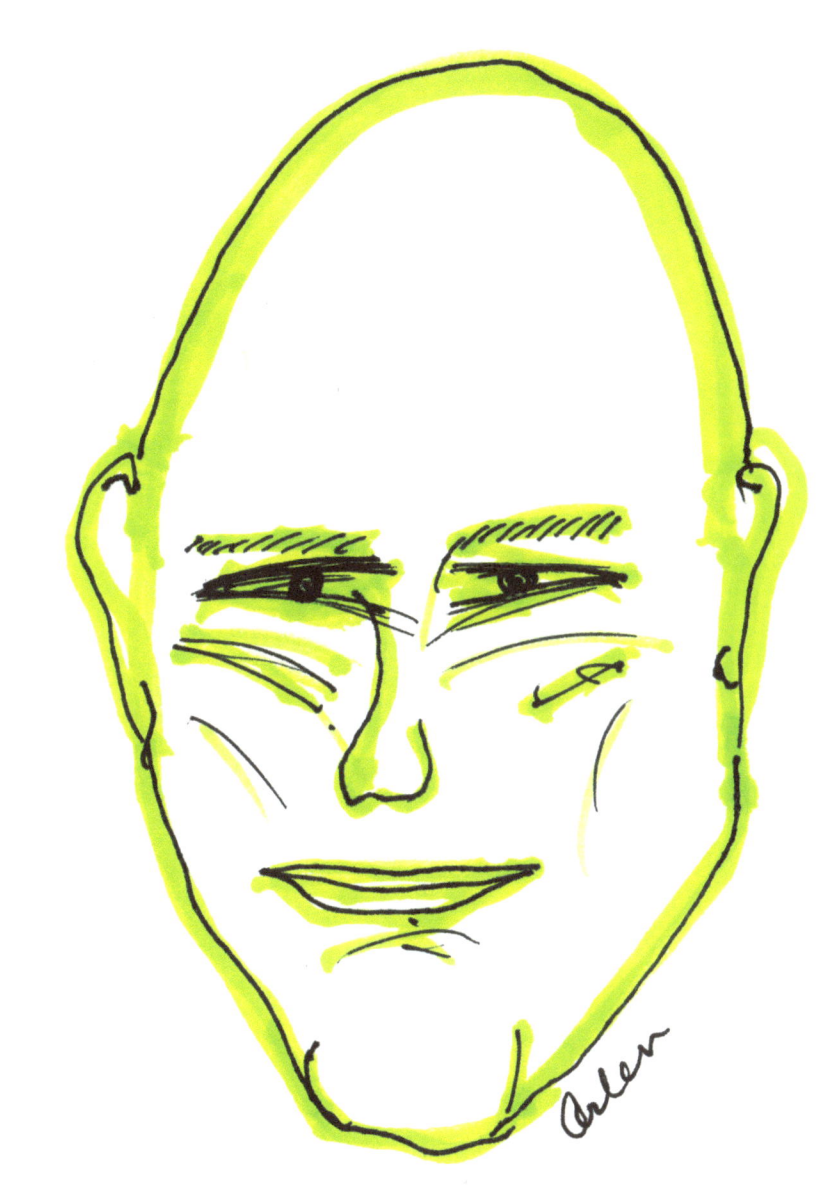

HUMAN TO ALIEN TRANSFORMATION
PHASE I

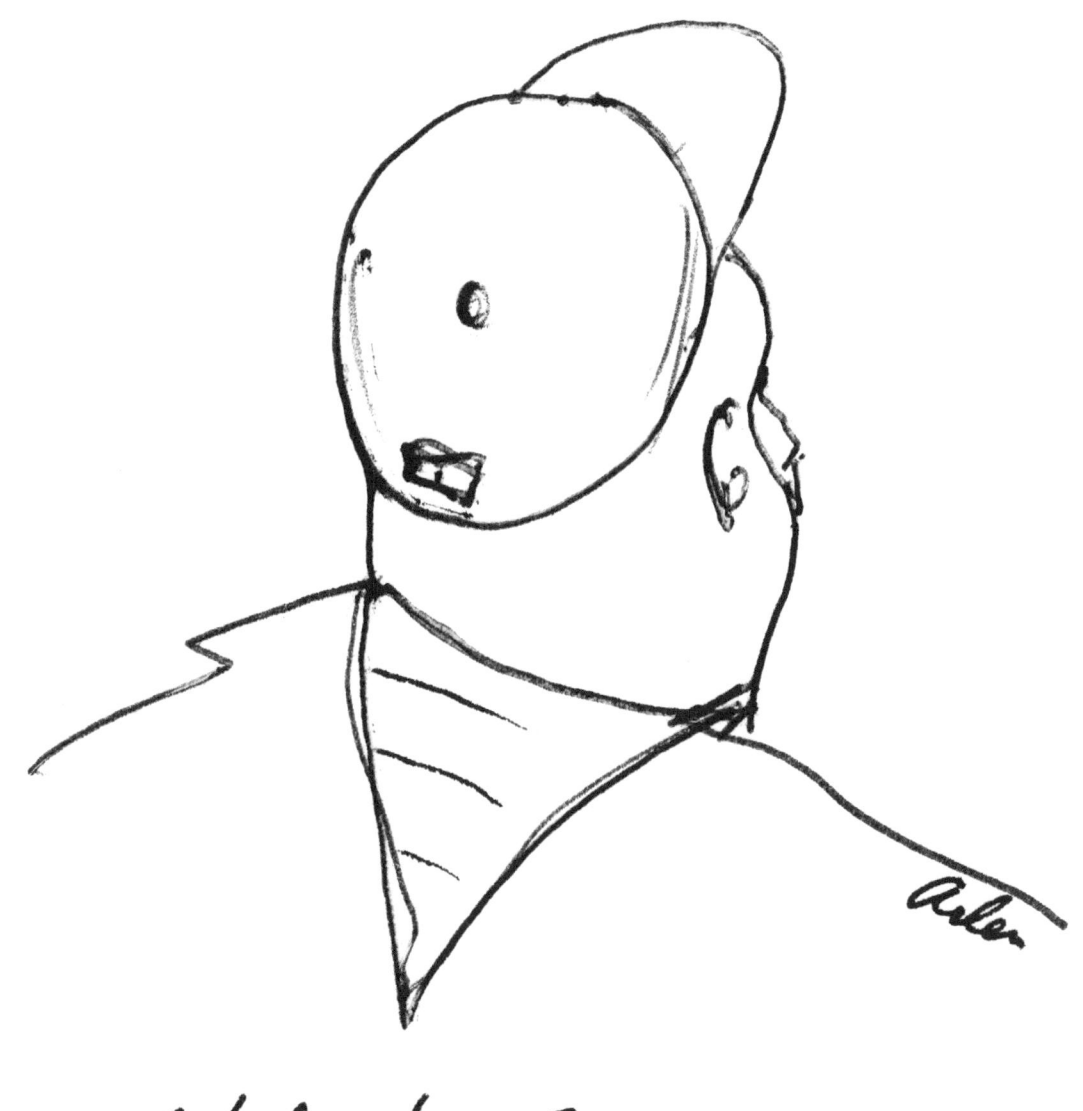

Oldest Scout

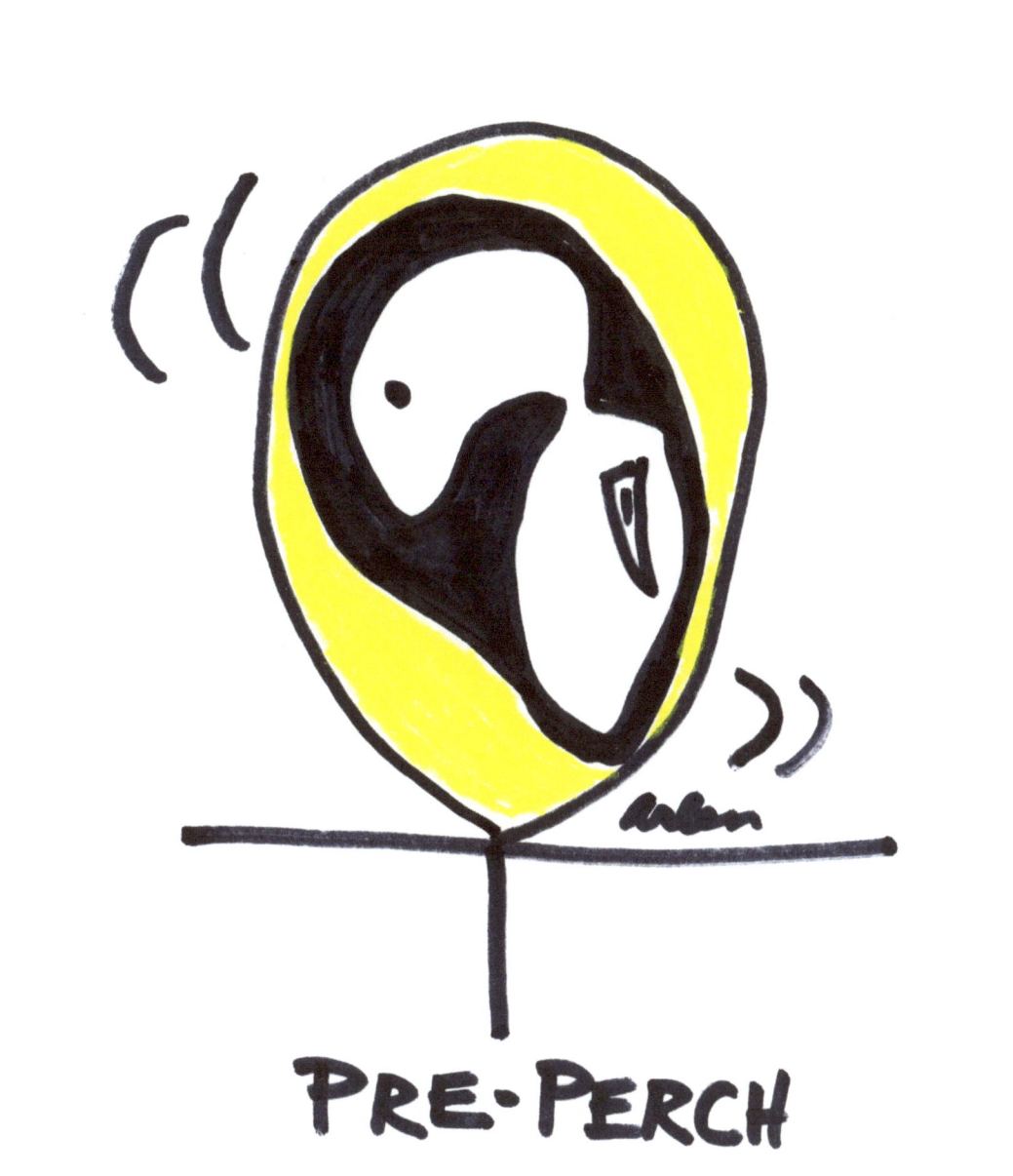

PRE-PERCH

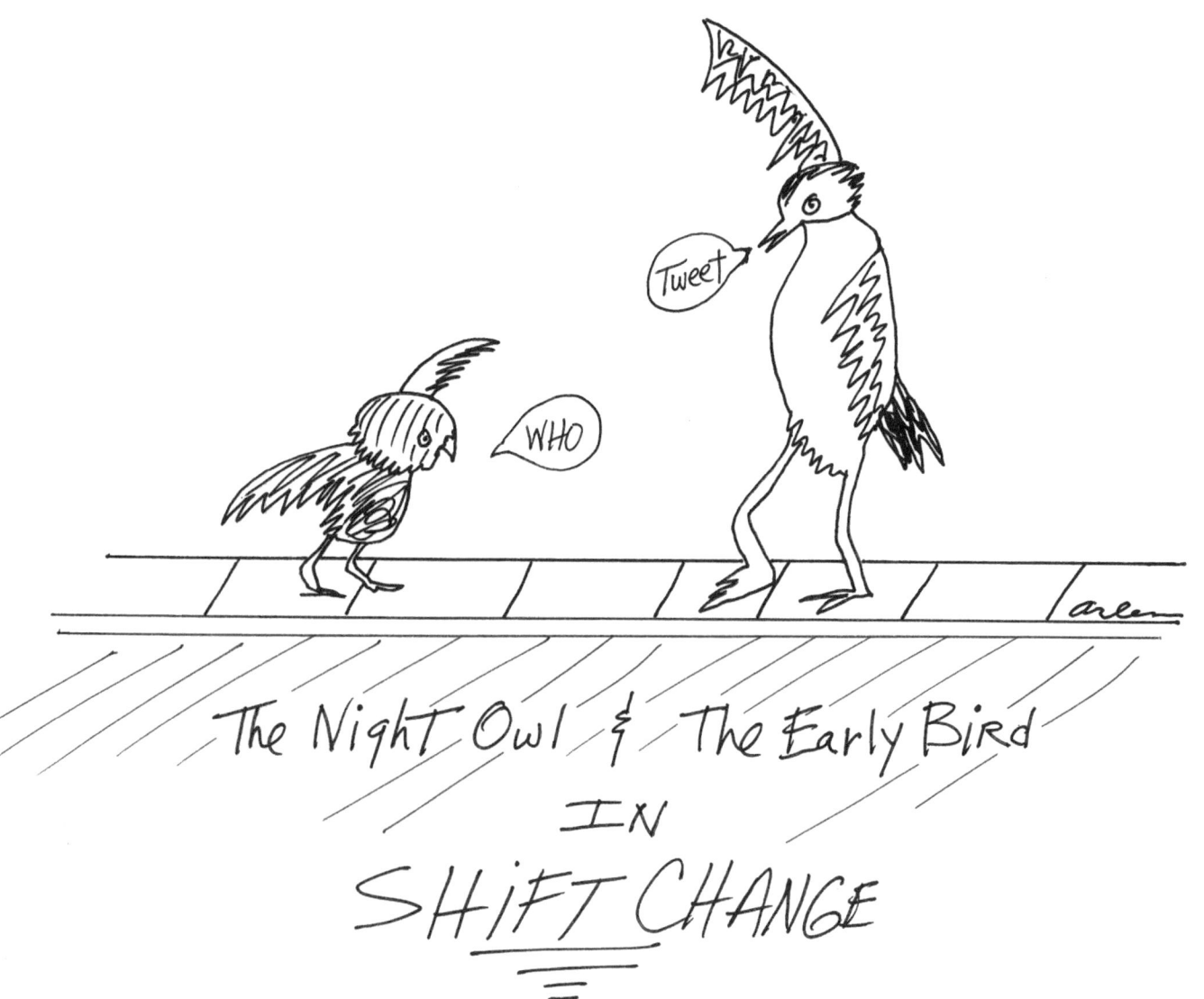

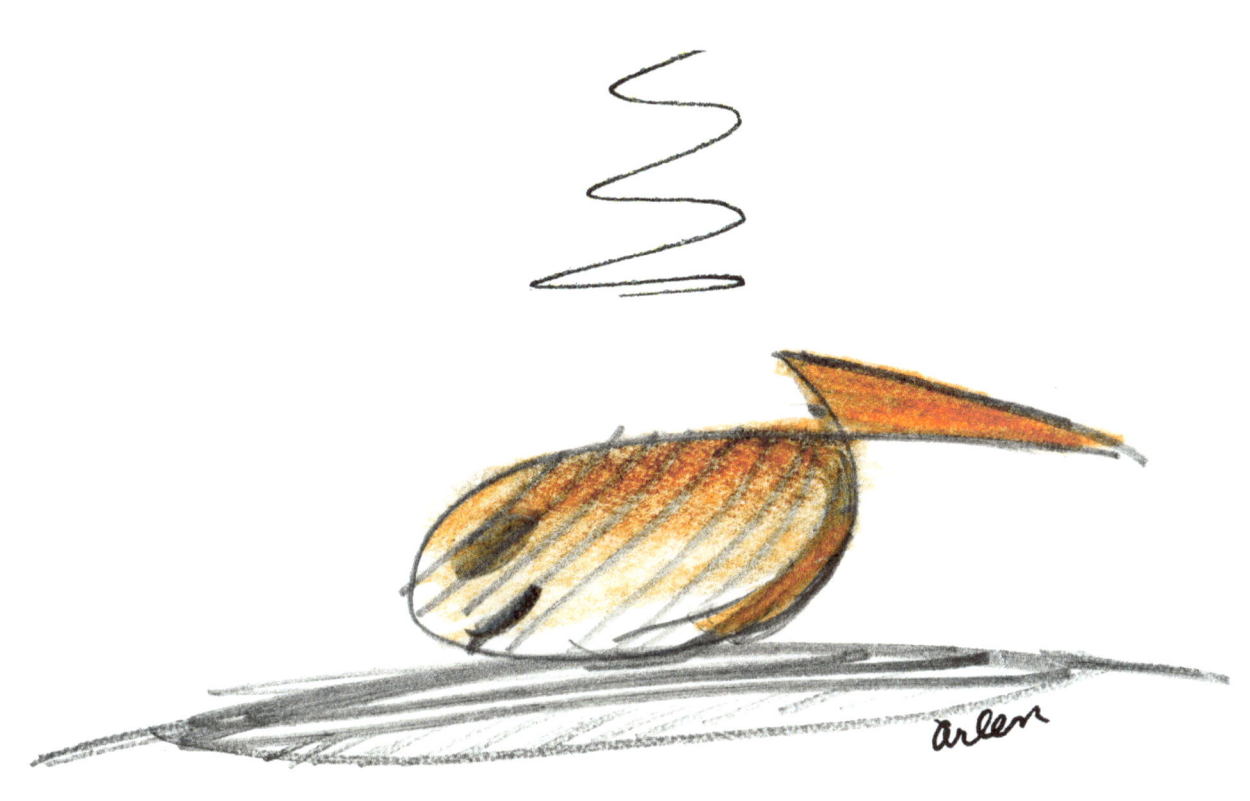

This Fish Refuses
To Die

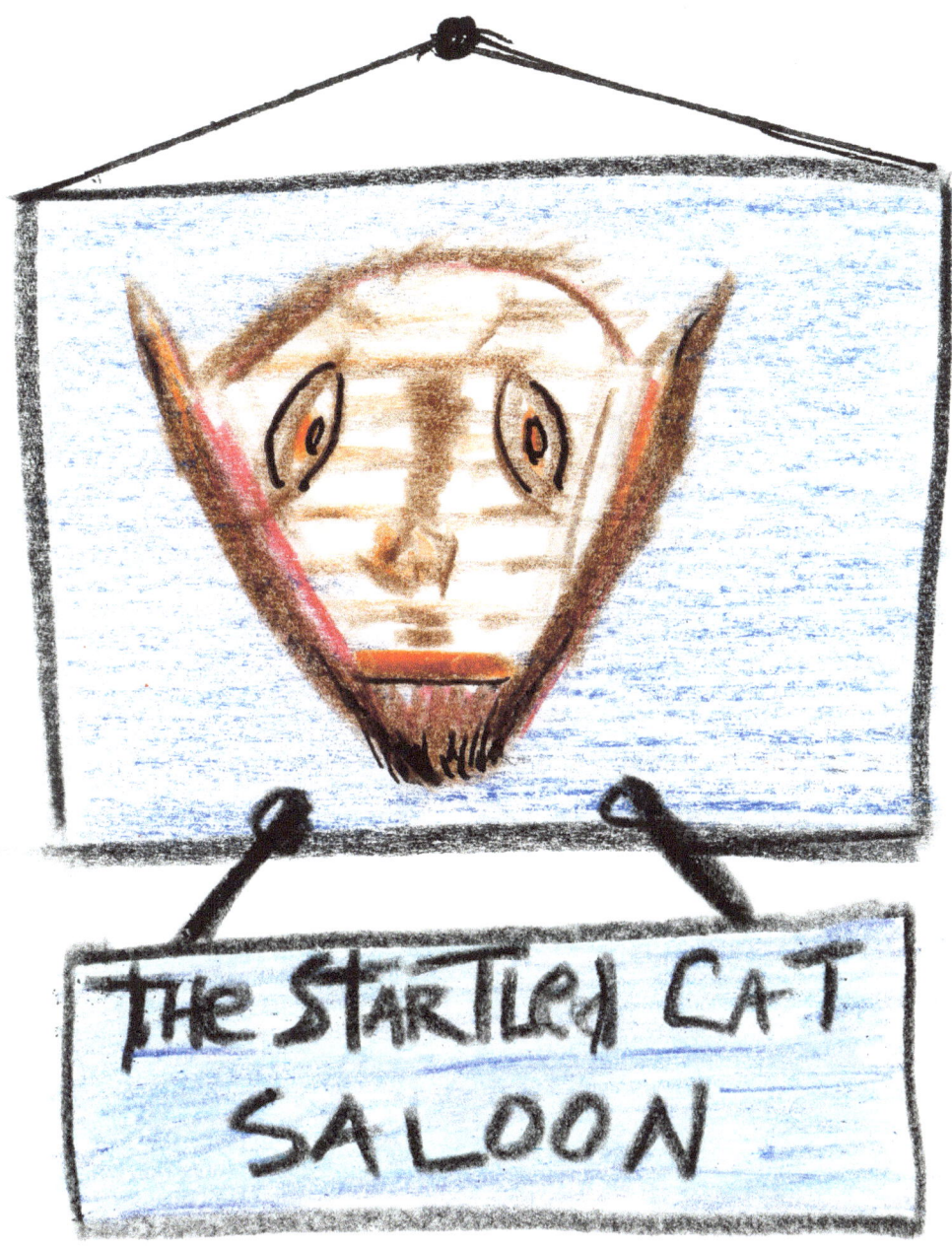

THE STARTLED CAT
SALOON

arlen

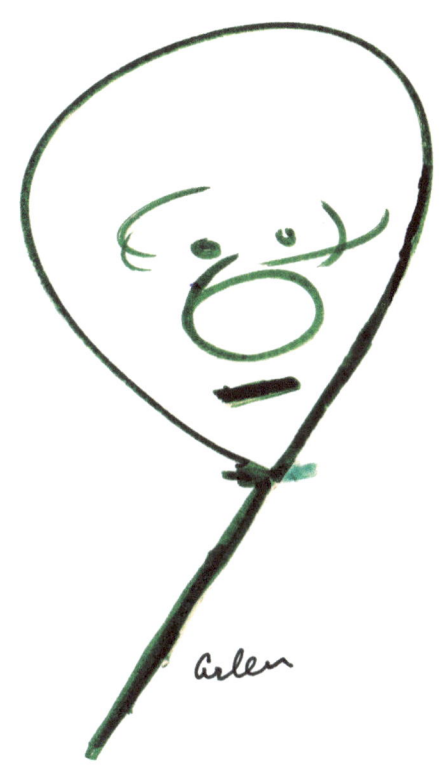

Balloon, STARTLED

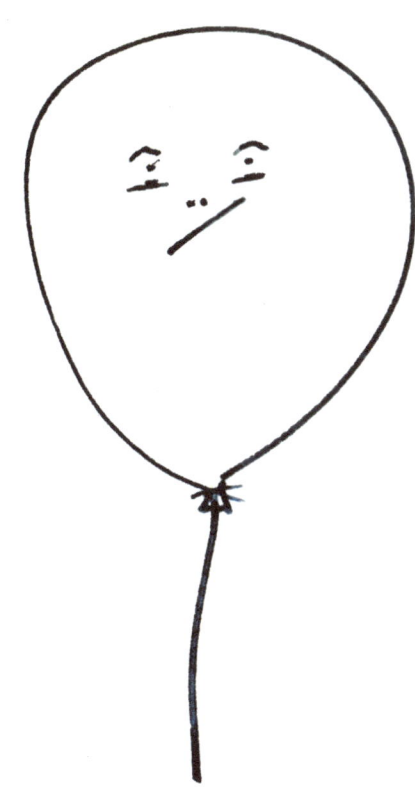

WISE-ASS BALloon

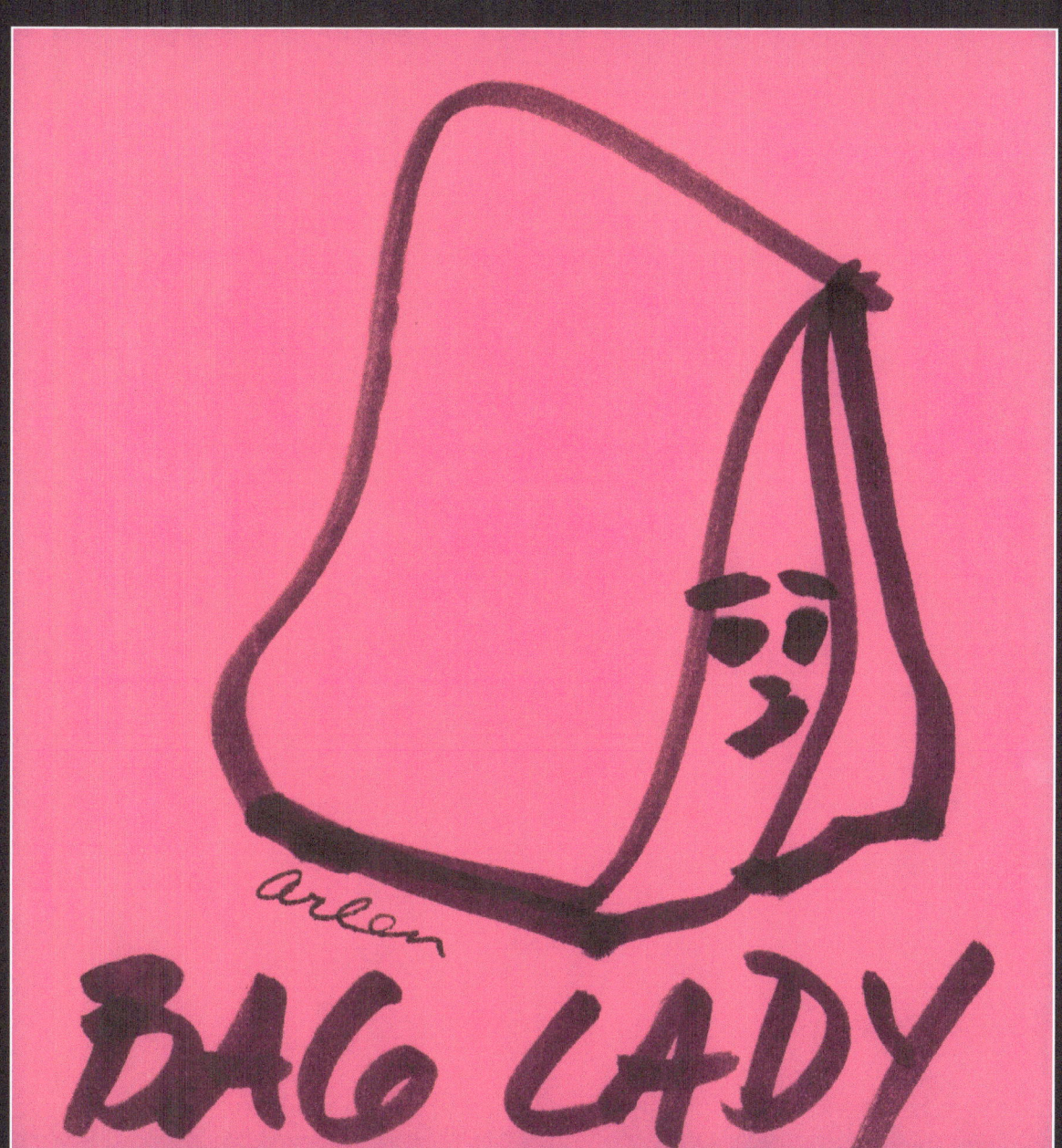

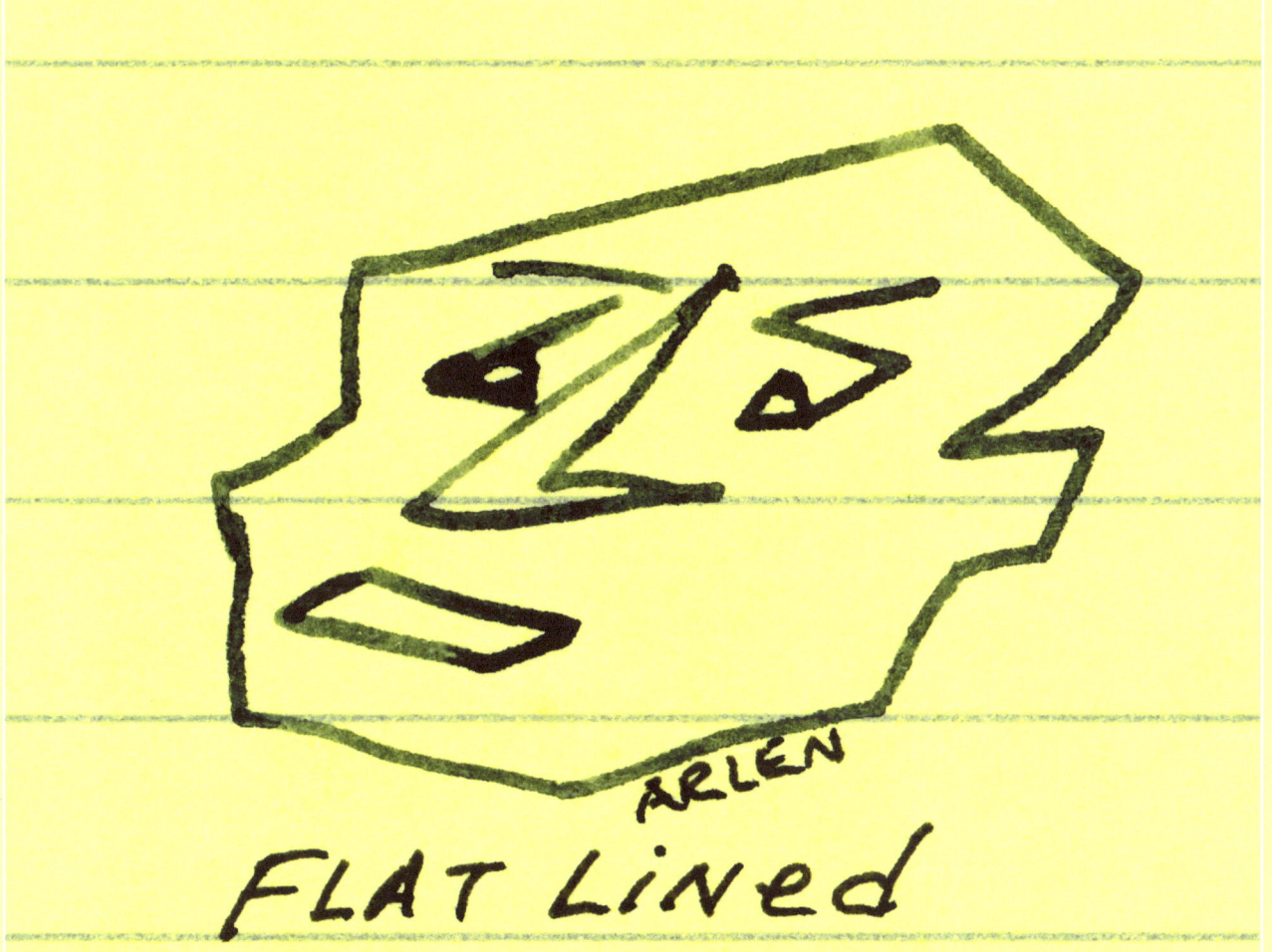

ARLEN

FLAT LineD

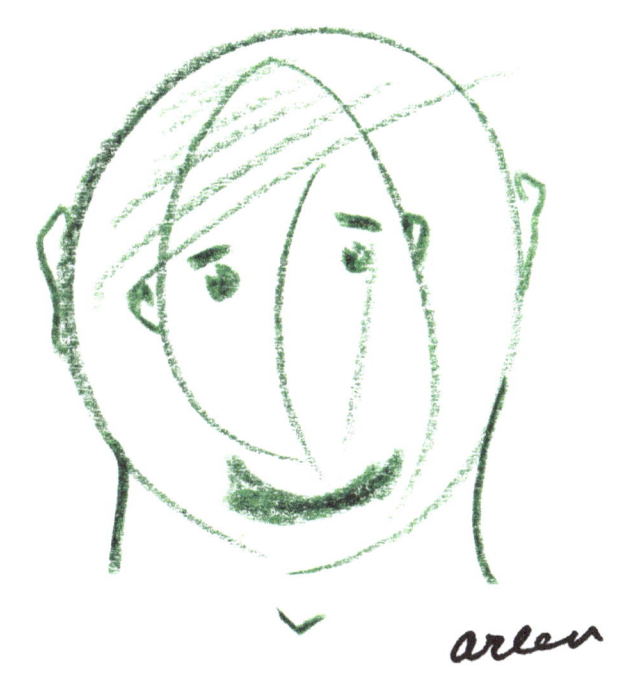

The MAN WithiN The MAN

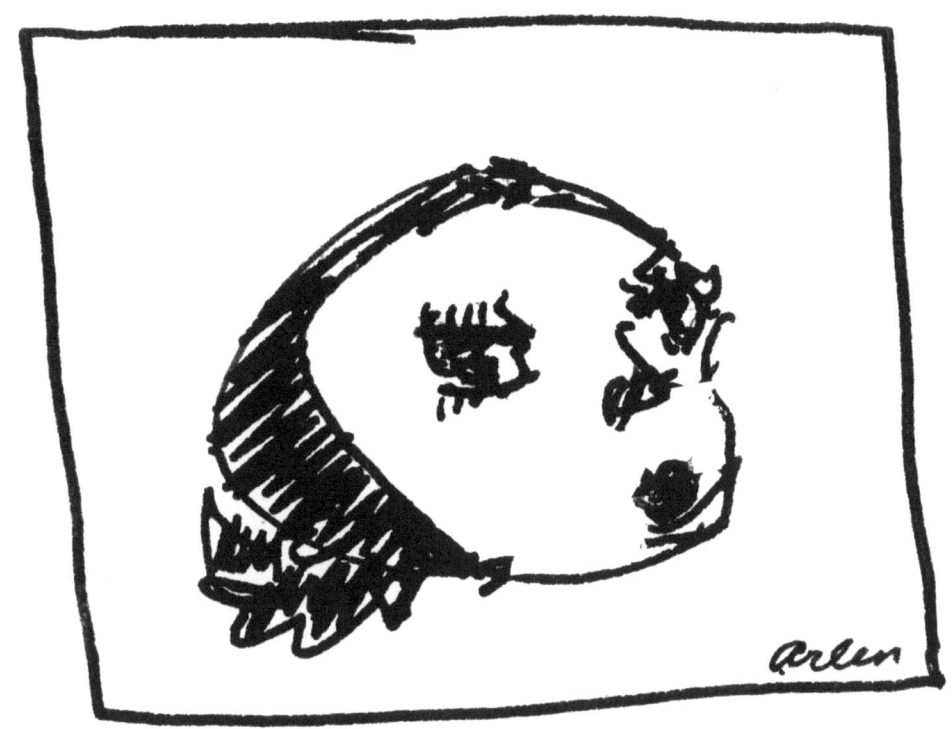

Letty Boop —
Betty's Sister

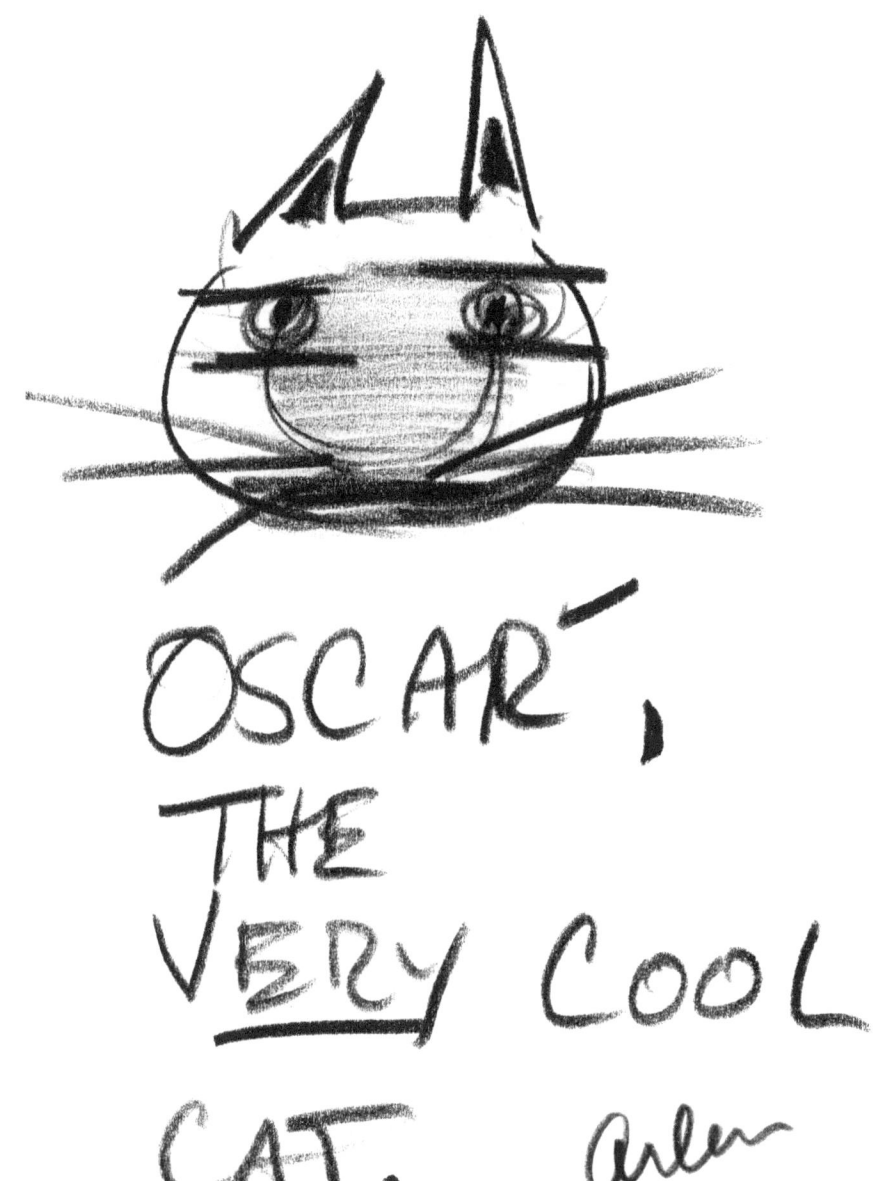

OSCAR,
THE
VERY COOL
CAT.

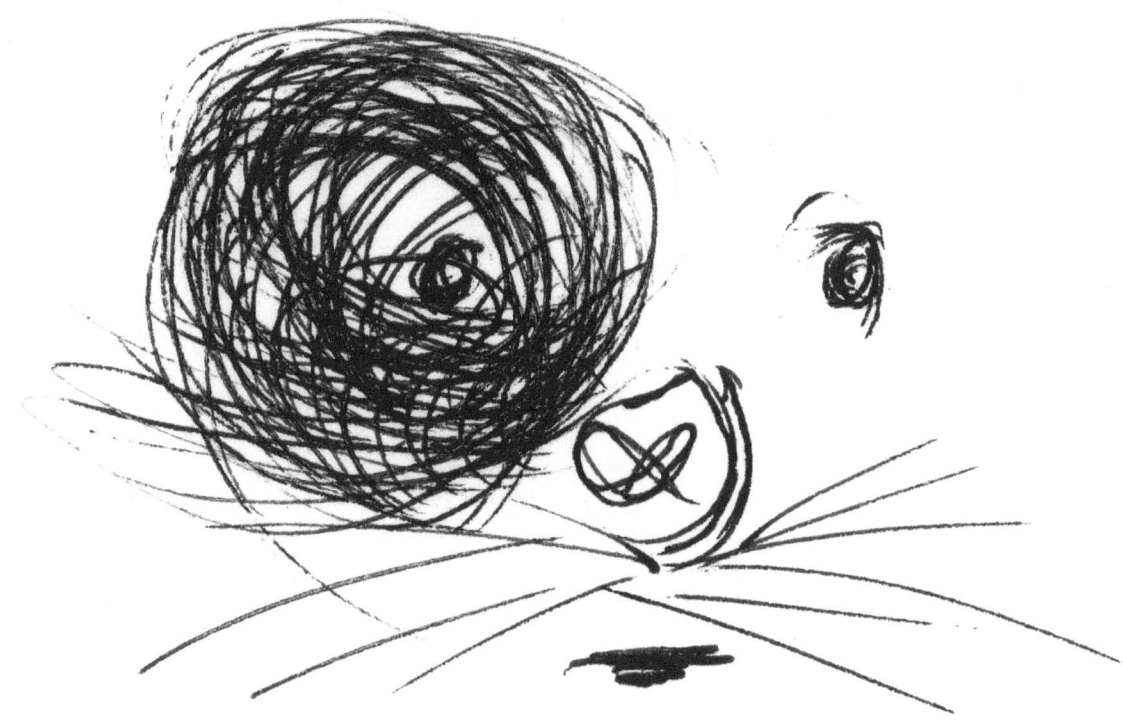

Cat or Mouse?
- Arlen

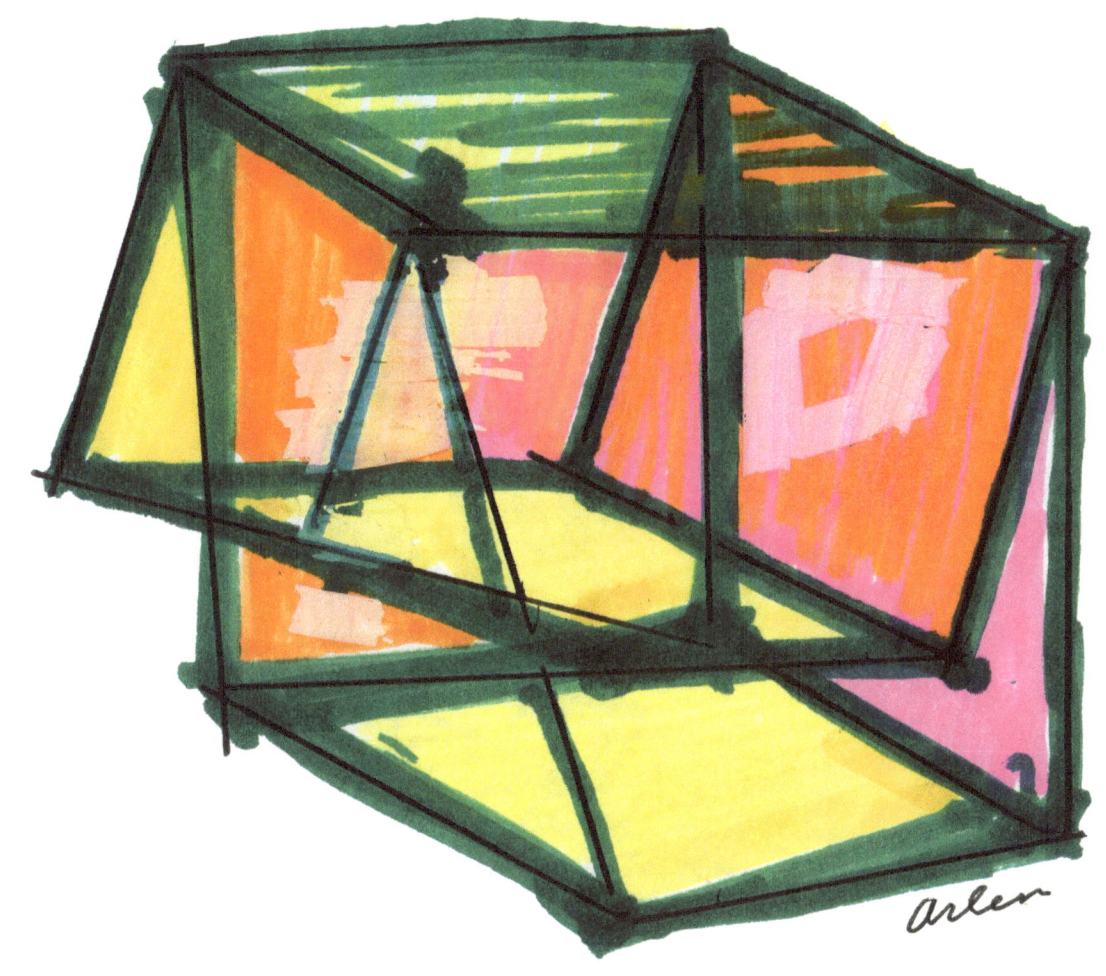

PICASSO'S CUFFLINK
BOX

arlen

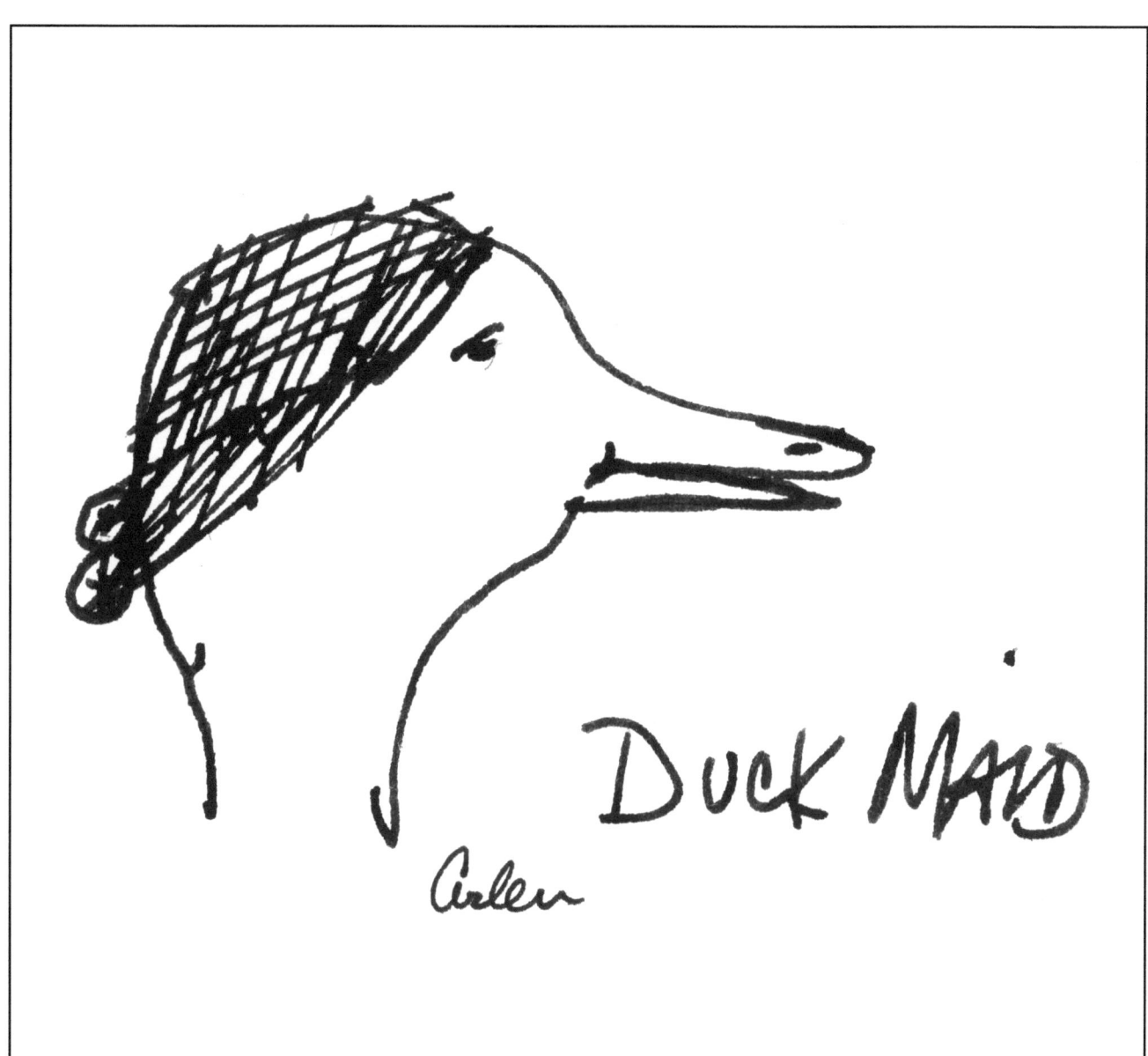

Duck Maid

Arlen

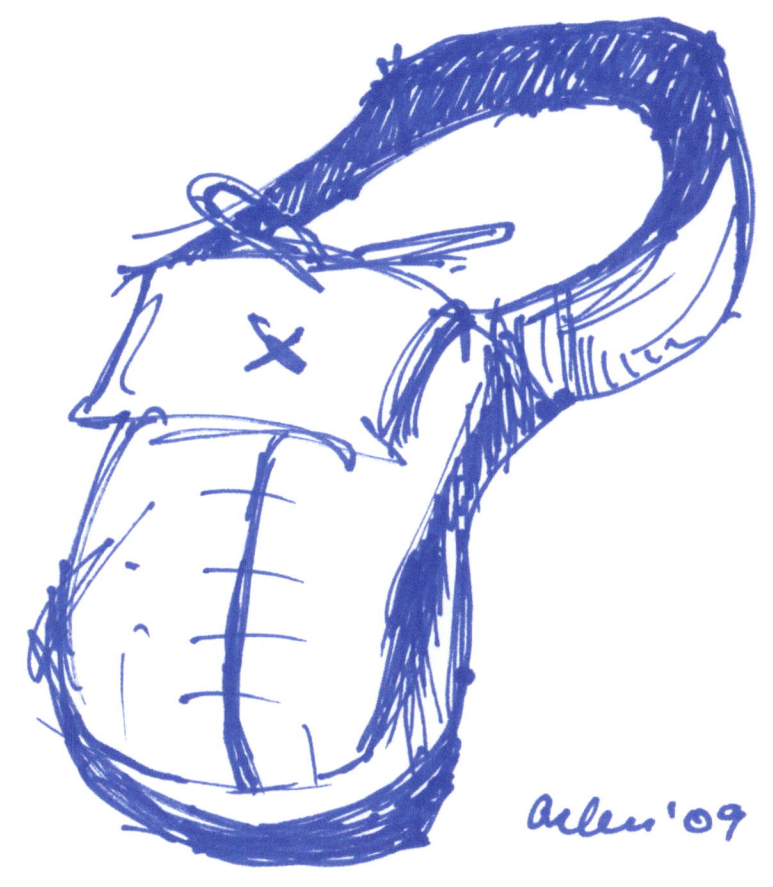

arlen '09

Joeless Shoe ——

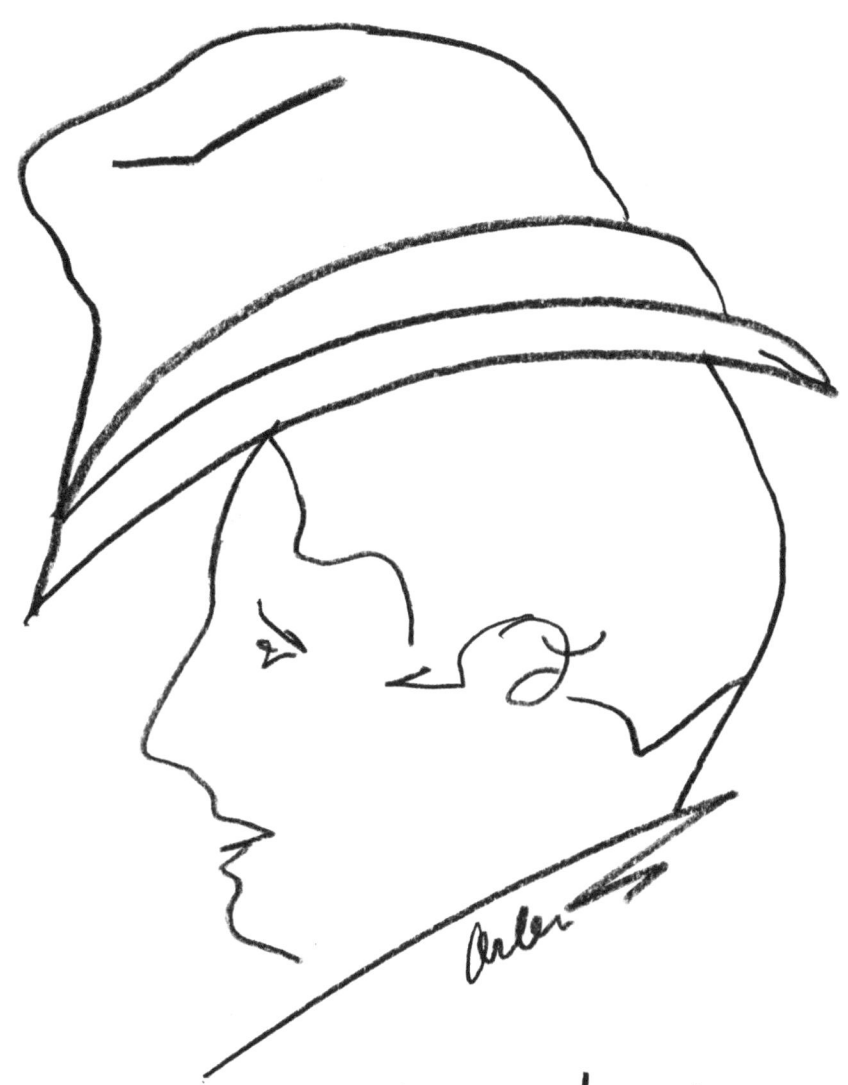

Winner Cocked Hat Contest

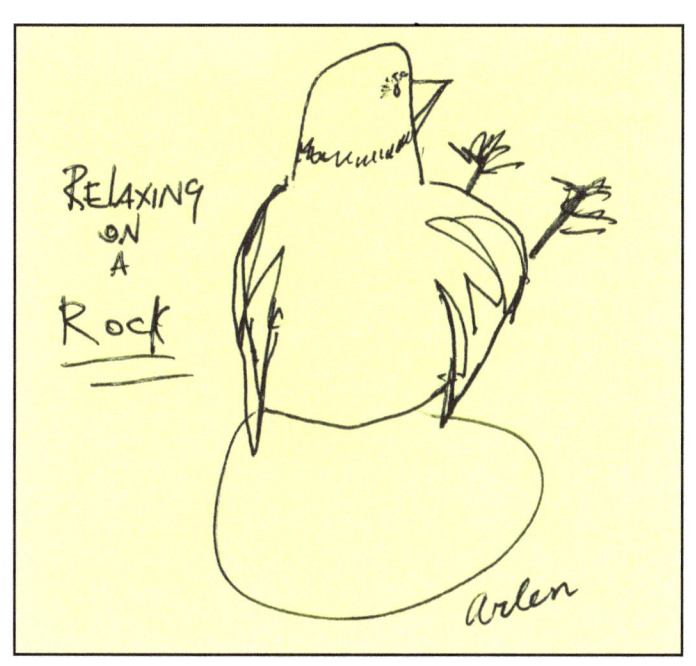

RELAXING ON A ROCK

arlen

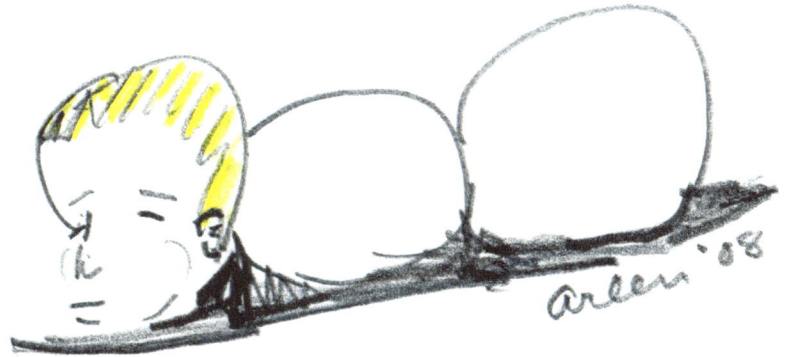

HEAD AMONGST THE ROCKS

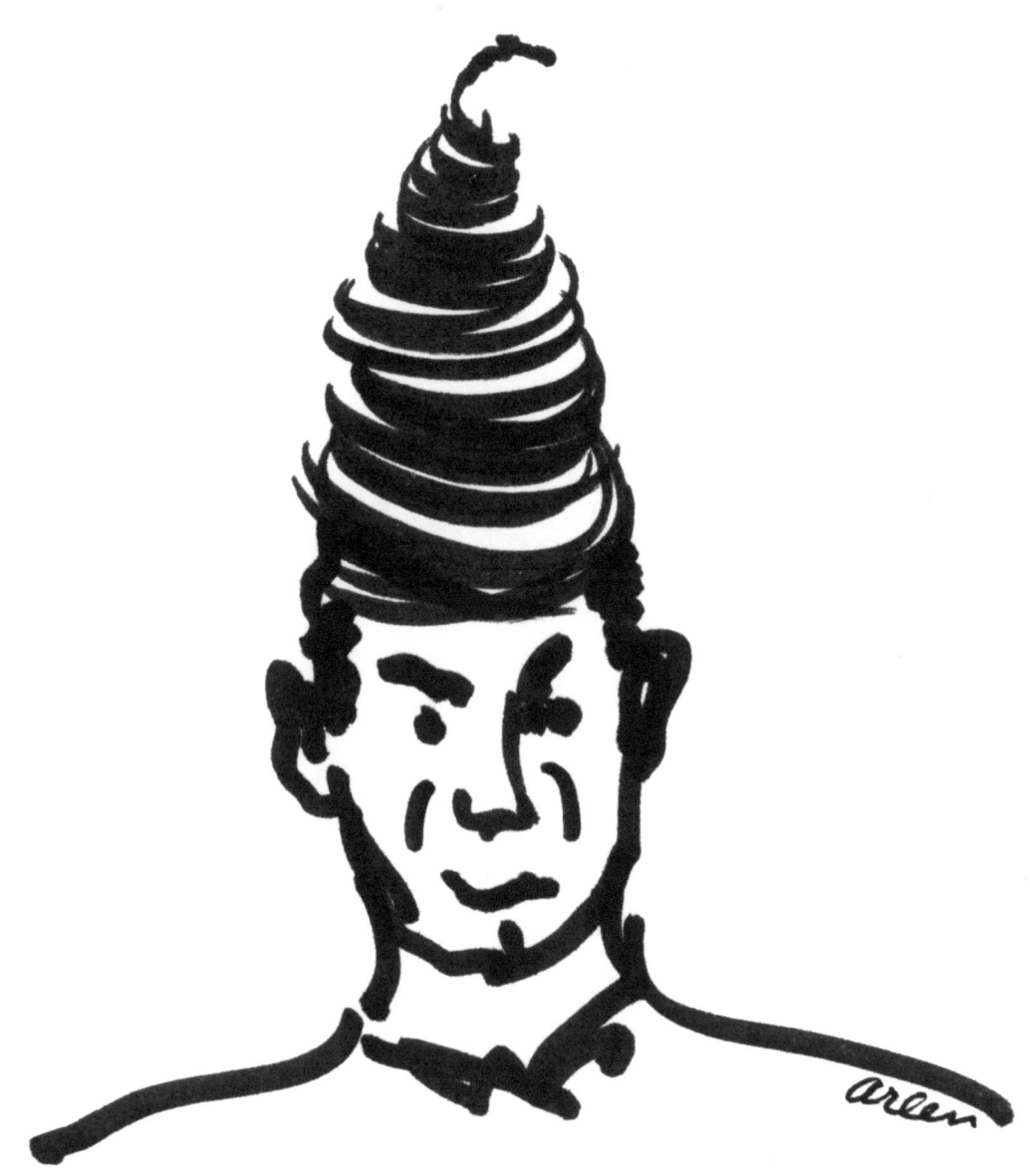

Local Potentate

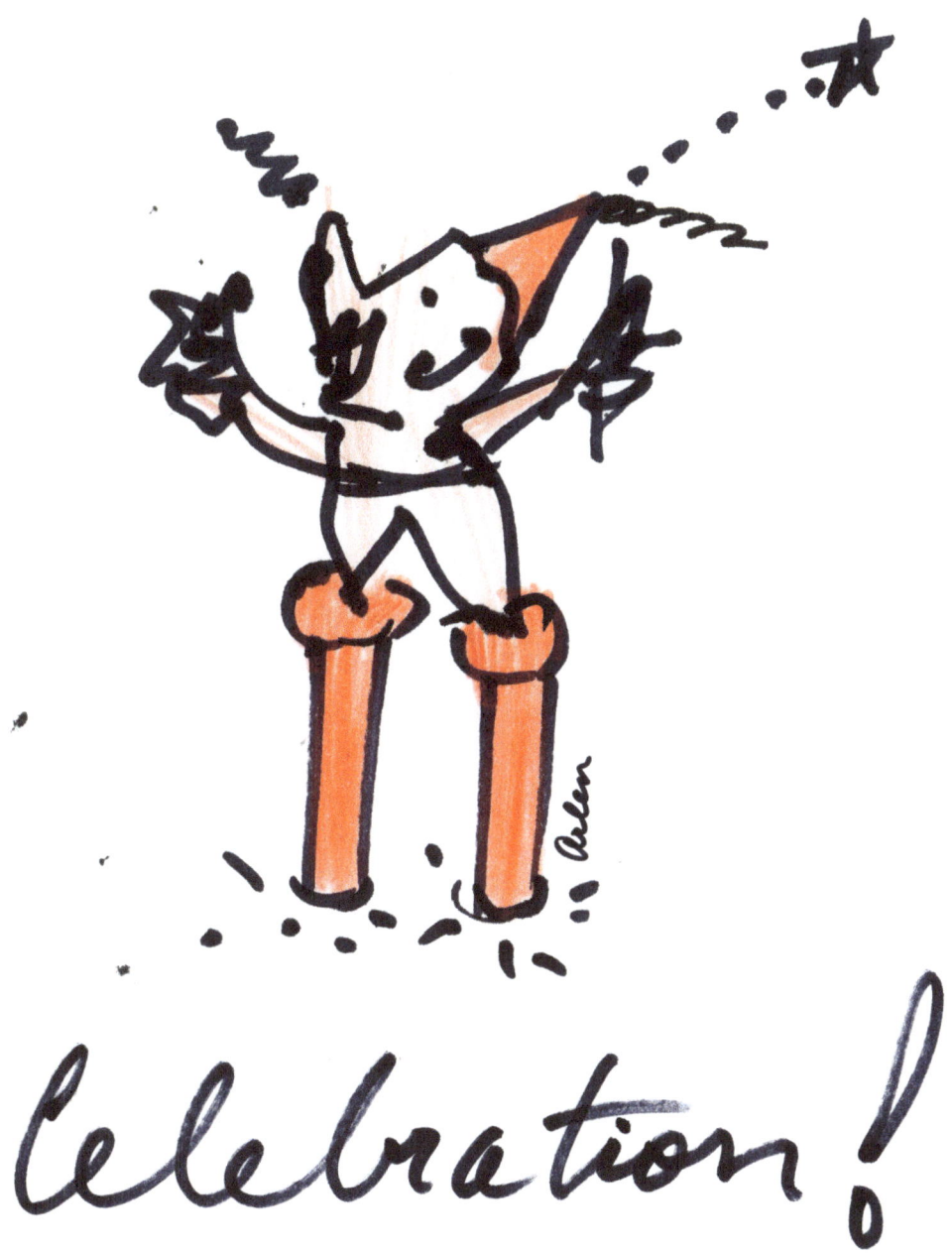

celebration!

THANK YOU for purchasing this book!

Please visit www.bamusers.com where
you can continue to be Bamused.

For book signings please contact
ArlenArts at email@arlenarts.com.

About the Author

Bruce Arlen has spent his career in the
graphic arts, advertising and design
industry, first representing and consulting
with one of the finest lithographers
in America and then as a partner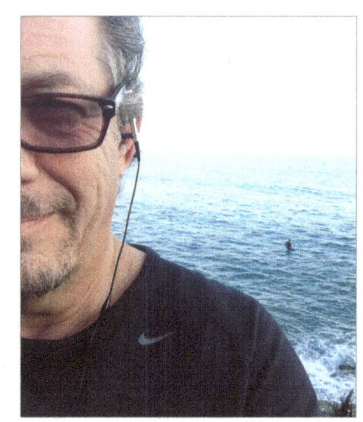
in a Los Angeles design, branding/identity and ad firm. In
that demanding world, Bruce produced countless projects for
hundreds of clients including Paramount Studios, Sony America,
Vidal Sassoon, Herbalife, FedEx Kinkos, Gallo Wineries, Honda,
and The Walt Disney Studios. Bruce now lives in Cave Creek,
Arizona, perched on the higher reaches of the Sonoran Desert,
where he continues to make art and conduct business.

www.ingramcontent.com/pod-product-compliance
Lightning Source LLC
Chambersburg PA
CBHW050720180526
45159CB00003B/1083